An open minded and open hearte   .. with a deep dark
past who ran away for years, fron ..mily tragedies, and found
peace in therapy.

I would like to dedicate this book to Dorothy Brough, my mother's eldest sister, my aunt, who was a great influence throughout my life. Her sense of humour, unlike her sisters, was a joy to me and much akin to my own. RIP Aunty Dorothy, you will be remembered forever, you were a legend. Xx

Also Julia Margaret Ellwood who was a constant friend throughout her life. Great fun, great friend, even though our ages were ten years apart, and sadly no longer with us.

And lastly, all the reps I worked with abroad who became the family that I had lost, even though they had no idea what I had gone through to drive me abroad. The great times we shared and the friendships and companionship. You saved my sanity better than any therapy and helped me enormously through a very troubled time. God Bless you all.

Howard Royston Potts

A MILE IN MY SHOES

A Travel Rep's Tale

AUSTIN MACAULEY PUBLISHERS™

LONDON • CAMBRIDGE • NEW YORK • SHARJAH

A CIP catalogue record for this title is available from the British Library.

ISBN 9781788488808 (Paperback)
ISBN 9781788780575 (Hardback)
ISBN 9781788781435 (ePub e-book)

www.austinmacauley.com

First Published (2021)
Austin Macauley Publishers Ltd
25 Canada Square
Canary Wharf
London
E14 5LQ

To Julia Margaret Ellwood, a truly great friend.

Introduction

Life is like a bus ride, people get on and off the bus throughout your life, some stay the whole journey and some just stay a short distance. Unfortunately, the first people to get off my bus were my parents! And I was only FIVE!

Hello and thank you for buying this book. I am Howard R Potts, the author, and I truly believe that my journey through life could inspire people to re assess their values and life goals. I was going to call this book 'A Journey in the Dark', as I spent most of my life oblivious to the realities of life. This was due to trauma and lack of parental guidance. Let's start by saying that every "life" is a journey and we all get a start in life, some better than others and some more privileged than others. Mine is a unique case and I will endeavour to keep ahead and inform you in the best way that I can, of my journey and its meaning.

I am unique in that I am completely open minded and have an enquiring mind, this manifests itself in that when I don't agree with someone's point of view, I don't dismiss it out of hand but try to see it from their point of view and understand why they feel that way. I am a typical Gemini, a communicator, like to have multiple tasks to keep me busy and amused; I live life to the absolute full. I thrive on new experiences and shy away from mundane repetitive situations, but I was originally a stay-at-home type before going off to college. I have to keep busy otherwise I get bored and start getting into trouble. A recent quote I heard summed me up perfectly. "I really tried to behave myself tonight but there were far too many other options!" I have a brilliant sense of humour and see fun in almost everything I do. I am extremely down to earth and the humour and tragedy of this book should take you to new levels of rapture and empathy. It covers my early years being brought up as an almost feral child in a small North of England Mining Village through to our life as a family in a new town, culminating in family tragedies and the break-up of family life as we knew it. My travels abroad and due to my diverse sense of humour the fun and good times which ensued. The switch in the tail comes when I returned to the UK and faced my demons and went into therapy and had all of my life's beliefs and aspirations altered beyond belief. The darkness became the light and I was empowered with a way to deal with the past, the demons and the idiots that were my parents.

Let me describe ME so that you can understand me as a character. I am a mild mannered, strong silent type, BUT I have another side which typifies me as a Gemini, twins, and double standards. I have a raucous sense of humour. My old friend Alison (God rest her soul) used to meet me at the door of her Pub, The Arden Arms at Atley Hill, North Yorks. She used to say to me, "I do hope you are going to behave yourself tonight Howard."

I always replied, "I don't think so Alison, that just wouldn't be me!" I have mostly throughout life, when having to decide between the Devil and The Deep Blue Sea, let the Devil take control. Far more exciting! I have never played it

"Safe" and much prefer to be naughty. I have never let it get too far a hold that I have upset people and I have never been in serious trouble through it.

From the onset of my life, I have always been wild and free. Left to roam the streets and countryside as a child was probably the cause, but effectively left me more independent and aware of the world around me. I hate the constraints people put on themselves and the rules that they need to surround themselves (to protect them). I am capable of anything I put my mind to, extremely independent and blunt with the truth. I can be very opinionated but only on subjects that I know back to front. Whilst I have extremely strong views on a lot of subjects, I don't ever feel the need to alter other people's views, unless challenged, and I always listen to other people's opinions in the chance that it may sway mine.

I have always galloped full tilt at things I want to do and have taken it "on the nose" if I mess up. I detest folk who fill their lives with "What if". When I was riding cross country, I would never have got over a fence if I was thinking "What if". Bite the bullet and go is my motto.

This book is a pragmatic view of life as I have known it. I have not set out to catalogue my life as a romantic notion but to give you, the reader, the chance to see my life in stages and get an insight as to who I am today. I have enjoyed almost every minute of it and have derived great fun out of most of the things I have done. I hope the journey will give you the same amount of fun too.

Throughout life, step by step, up the emotional ladder you go, every hardship and blow, whether it be death, parting, abuse, abandonment, pushing you one step higher. And once you acquire new height, you have to look down on the poor people below you on the ladder, who have never endured what you have, but they will all have an opinion as to what YOU should do. Frustrating as it is. YOU have the higher enlightenment, the ability to walk away and not listen to them, A greater understanding and a broader outlook. Give thanks that you are not a poor person anymore. Give thanks that you can use your gift to help others, should you so wish. My book was written just after Therapy so it is brutal in its honesty and provided me with a way to make a BIG PICTURE of the factors which made me into the strong character that I am today. I make no apologies for the wrongs that shaped me into what I have become today, and likewise I hold no grudges. But I admit, I have cut myself off from the caustic, selfish family who, to this day, do not understand my plight. They remain the plastic people that they always were. Bereft of shame, responsibility and reality, and most of all, any INTEGRITY! This is my life in a book. Nothing can change the events that warranted me writing it. I have done the time, but I didn't do a crime. The rage, the depression and the emotion have all gone now, life is sweet again.

My Life Plot

1955. June 9 – I was born in Hardwick Hall Sedgefield.

1956. Age 1 – Alan born, October 26th

1957. Age 2

1958. Age 3 – Neville born, 20th March

1959. Age 4 – Started at Fishburn Infants School. Carolyn born, 18th March.

1960. Age 5.

1961. Age 6

1962. Age 7

1963. Age 8 – Moved to Fishburn Junior Mixed School.

1964. Age 9

1965. Age 10 – Moved to Newton Aycliffe. Stephenson Way Junior School.

1966. Age 11 – Started at Marlowe Hall Secondary School.

1967. Age 12

1968. Age 13

1969. Age 14 – Moved to Woodham Comprehensive School, Newton Aycliffe.

1970. Age 15

1971. Age 16 – Started a year's practical work at Snipe House Farm, Darlington.

1972. Age 17 – Went to Durham Agricultural College (2 years).

1973. Age 18

1974. Age 19

1975. Age 20 – Started work at Carrsides Farm

1976. Age 21

1977. Age 22 – Father walked out on us, Christmas Eve.

1978. Age 23

1979. Age 24 – Neville killed on 29th Sept.

1980. Age 25

1981. Age 26

1982. Age 27 – Spain – summer / Austria – winter

1983. Age 28 – Spain – summer / Austria – winter.

1984. Age 29 – Athens for ILG (Intasun – Training Course).

1985. Age 30 – Crete – summer / Agadir – winter.

1986. Age 31 – Crete – summer / Benidorm – winter.

1987. Age 32 – Crete – summer / Gibraltar – winter.

1988. Age 33 – Rhodes – summer / Gibraltar – winter. Holiday to India.

1989. Age 34 – Israel / Rhodes – summer. Holiday to Barbados (twice).

1990. Age 35 – Israel / Thassos – summer. Holiday to USA. (*Benidorm*).

1991. Age 36 – London

1992. Age 37 – London

1993. Age 38 – London

1994. Age 39 – Moved to Cleasby, North Yorkshire (May).

1995. Age 40

1996. Age 41

1997. Age 42

1998. Age 43

1999. Age 44

2000. Age 45

Chapter 1

Early Years

I have always been wild, brought up wild, have a wild sense of humour and thrive on the freedom it gives me. The injustices of my life have driven me to be wilder. Wild is a way of life, a lifestyle and it empowered me with the survival skills needed in an ever-changing world. I was never meant for a safe world. I would be bored out of my head and I really don't have time in life for this sort of person and have quickly moved on from any encounters with them. (Madge, my mother, was boring to the extreme.)

Let me introduce myself. I am Howard Royston Potts. I was born on 9th June 1955 in the Hardwick Hall at Sedgefield in the North of England. This great big country house had been commissioned as a Maternity Home during the war and was still operating as such. Our family lived in Fishburn, the next village to Sedgefield. I am the second of five children and the eldest son to Marjorie and Roy Potts. I don't want to say too much about myself as you will get to know me gradually throughout this book. I would just like to mention at this point that the delusions of grandeur my mother must have had calling me Howard Royston Potts, it's quite a title for some little tyke from a small mining village. I don't complain though as it has got me into some exclusive clubs and social circles in my time, and as a result I have developed my intellectual tastes. My life has been an adventure and I can never be classed as a boring old conformist. I have a big heart, a very open mind and a lust for knowledge and travel equal to none. I have never wanted to conform and I am very spontaneous in my actions. I do it and then pay the consequences later. I live life to the full. My biggest asset is my sense of humour and the ability to make people laugh. I see fun in everything I do, including funerals! Innuendo and double entendre are my favourite types of humour. I am also extremely down to earth and speak as I find. My motto in life is, if you can't stand the truth, then don't stand next to me!

My immediate Family consists of:

Mother, Marjorie, I used to call her Madge when I got older, she hated it. I shall refer to her as such from here onwards as a mark of total disrespect to her and her lack of interest in my wellbeing. (The reasons behind this will become apparent when you read through the rest of this book.) My saying for her was, if you expect nothing from my mother, you get it in abundance! She used to work in the family Post Office when she left school and then went off to join The Wrens where she met my father. Like her mother she was Big Boned and spent her time cooking and cleaning for her family. She used to bake, scones, rock cakes, tarts etc, once a week. In later life I heard the saying that only dull boring women have clean houses, that was her! No hobbies, apart from stuffing her face, watching TV and cleaning. She had no sense of humour, unlike Aunty Dorothy, her sister, absolutely no sense of adventure and no back bone. She pampered to her needs before her family and was small minded to the extremes. We would taunt her in our teenage years by asking her, "The blue vein on my willy is getting bigger, what does that mean?" She would be mortified. I lay on the carpet in front of the TV one night and lit a fart for her to see, it went off with a brilliant blue and yellow flame. All she could say was, "You daft bugga, you'll set fire to the carpet!"

We could come home from school to cornflakes for our tea but she could still afford to smoke and the dog would be having chicken. What a mix of priorities. Our suffering at her hands was, as children we got smacked, then the belt, then the hearth brush. In later years we got the riding crop, thumped or kicked. This all stopped when I was 18 and having been in the bath with the radio on, she waited outside the door until I came out with a towel around my waist and she slapped me so hard on my bare flesh. I saw red and hit her so hard that she nearly fell down the stairs. She never hit me again. The negativity this woman put into our life was enormous. We weren't important. She came first in everything. She used to have a stash of sweets, cakes and biscuits hidden in pans and hiding places, just for her. I remember at 4 years old coming in from playing and seeing her ironing and sucking a sweet. "Have you got some sweets?" I asked.

"No, I am just sucking my tongue," she replied.

At 18, I wanted to buy my first car but I was short of £200, Father said he would loan me it and I promised to pay him back within two weeks. She stepped in and told me that I couldn't have the money as she wanted to go on holiday. So, being defiant, I got a loan from the bank and bought it. Guess who was the first to ask for lifts here and there in it? I really don't want you, as the reader, to think that these petty demeanours should colour your judgement of my mother.

Keep all your judgement until the end of this book when you can make a proper assessment of her character.

Father Roy, he was from Abbey Hulton, Stoke on Trent, and had been a messenger boy after leaving school but went on to join The Fleet Air Arm. He came from a family of five, four boys and a girl. He was the youngest so got spoilt. After he married my mother, he worked hard at Neecol in Ferryhill, a village not far away. He was a Foreman Steel Erector. We didn't see that much of him in our early years as he went to work early and came back late. We used to meet him on the path when he got home so we could to see if he had left us any bait (his sandwiches). Looking back, he was the Victorian father who would arrive back from work for my mother to tell him stories of what we had been up to and he would punish us.

He loved himself and would preen himself in front of the mirror. He used Brylcream on his hair and would slick it back, well it was very '50s' Rock & Roll in those days. He worked hard and would come home to 5, Maughan Terrace, drop his bags and disappear up to the pit baths to get cleaned up. We didn't have a bath in the house! Mother used to bath the kids in the kitchen sink. On a couple of occasions, I had to go to work with him. I would sit in his van with a packet of sweets or something to amuse me. The worst bit was having to get up so early and have breakfast cooked by him. He would make porridge with water and salt, Mother always made it with sugar and milk; He would only toast bread on one side. Yuck! His biggest problem in life was his temper. Shit would fly for the smallest of excuse. I have seen the Sunday dinner fly up the walls of the kitchen just because Mother dared to feed us before he got back in from the pub. What a He Man!

Christine Sandra the eldest daughter, she maimed us all in one way and another when we were kids. She split my eyebrow open, not sure how but I still have the scar. She knocked one of Alan's teeth out, I think she had him in his pushchair and was scooting it along with one foot on the axle and upended him. I can't remember what else she did to the other two but she was the eldest and she was the boss. She wore National Health glasses that resembled jam jar bottoms, so my name for her was the goggly eyed nit of the world. As young as we were at Maughan Terrace I remember getting milk and biscuits for supper one night, and she got the hump cos she had broken ones. She stole one of mine and I told her then that I would remember for the rest of my life that she stole the wrong biscuit! She was a bugga for fighting and if we had to walk to or from school with her, we had to put up with her brawls. There was a girl called Audrey lived around the corner from us at Moorside Cres. Christine could not abide the sight of her. She would beat the shit out of her in the gutter and the next thing her mother would be round our house to tell Madge. We learned that we hadn't to have much respect for Audrey's mother so we used to shout abuse at her from the street. She would shout back that we were all "cheeky fond".

Then there is me, Howard, the eldest son.

Alan Geoffrey came along 18 months after me. Bright ginger hair that Mother used to curl around a brush on top of his head. It resembled a chicken's comb. I used to fight like hell with him. I even got him down on the ground and jumped up and down on him, and that was before I was 5. I hated him. We had to share a bunk bed for a while, top and tail, and I used to tell him that he wasn't to touch me and kicked him like hell.

James Neville (we always called him Neville) came along approximately 18 months after Alan. He was a little blonde thing and we all looked after him. He loved nature and would walk miles with his little dog, Penny, a Yorkshire Terrier. He eventually became a carpenter and worked at a shop in Darlington restoring antiques. He would make furniture in his spare time in the garage at home. Bedside tables, tables etc. He was collecting old copper pennies as he planned to make a table and inlay them on the top. Like me he loved soul music and disco music and would listen to it constantly.

Carolyn Ann came along last of all, a little doll with a shock of white blonde hair,

Gran used to call her Topsy as she was so doll like. I remember the day she was born at home, Father wanted to call her Debra. YUK! I had never heard this name before. Luckily for her they called her Carolyn Ann which really should have been Caroline Ann after some family friend's daughter.

We had close family living around us in Fishburn. My mother's elder sister, Dorothy, lived up the road from us in a caravan with Uncle Len in the back of a cow pasture splattered with cow pats. You had to climb over the style on the main road opposite The Beehive Pub and almost do hopscotch, through the cowpats, across the field to the caravan. She eventually moved around the corner from us when we moved to our second house. Aunty Dorothy had been in The Wrens with my mother and she loved to dance so it was natural progression that she married Len Brough, from Sedgefield, who was the drummer in a band. Aunty Dorothy was, and still is, a great laugh.

See page 7.

Aunty Dorothy

Dorothy and Len eventually moved out of their caravan up the village and moved into a house in Oakdene Road, which was just along the street from where we lived in Moorside Crescent. Uncle Len had a motorbike which he kept in a shed in the garden. It was quite a thing to have in those days as there were hardly any cars on the roads. I used to pop round to see him tinkering with the engine and shining up the chrome bits. He also had his drum kit in the living room and I had drumming lessons off him.

Dorothy worked in the kitchens at the General Hospital so when we went out for a walk past there, we would shout through the kitchen door and she would bring us ice creams. When I was in hospital, she really was a God send, bringing me food, sweets and ice cream. I saw more of her than I did my own parents.

If we had to use their toilet, we used to run along the street nearly cross legged and bang on the back door and tell Aunty Dorothy we needed to use her toilet. (It was never a loo in those days.) If she was already using it, she would shout through the door for us to Piss Off! Crude we know, but that is how it was in those days.

If Dorothy babysat for us, we would get the record player out and blast the living room with music, and dance around the room. She really was the opposite to our mother. Best aunty, best friend, and great fun to be around. We used to tell her dirty jokes and she would play soppy stern, but her face gave her away, because her eyes were laughing. If you told her another one, she would bark, "You are there again!"

She had one daughter, Elaine, who we would take out for a walk in her pushchair around the lanes. Aunty Dorothy would know in an instant when we got back if we had taken her out of the pushchair, which we normally did to sit on the grass down by the Cricket field.

Dorothy and Len eventually split up and Dorothy broke her heart. She used to tell us when we were teenagers that she had to get on top of Len and help herself to get our Elaine. She remained on her own for the rest of her life.

In later years Dorothy came to Crete with Madge to visit me. I had a motorbike, a Honda 350cc with drop handlebars. Dorothy was straight on the back behind me and flying around the streets of Agios Nikolaos, up and down the steep hills, she loved it.

My grandmother, Sarah Ethel Jopling, Nee Walton (Etty), lived in Sedgefield in a lovely '30s' semi-detached house in Spring Lane with Uncle Arnold Jopling, who was the brother of her second husband. Her house was always immaculate. She had a brown leather sofa and chairs which she polished with wax and you slid off if you weren't careful. She was a big woman and if my memory serves me well, she was 72 inches around the hips. (I cannot remember where I got that from.) When she bent over to poke the fire, her stockings and her bloomers (long pants) didn't meet up, so the sight of her stocking tops and an enormous amount of lardy white, veiny flesh before her bloomer legs was a constant source of amusement to us lads. She was a character and a half. She would sing along to songs on the TV in a beautiful soprano voice. If you saw her down the street in Sedgefield, she would be dressed to the nines with a hat with a hat pin, immaculate coat and as she had been in business, she knew almost everyone in the village. At home, well that was a different story. She had a turn of phrase that used to make us laugh.

"My God lad, you want to know the far end of a fart and which way the stink blows" if we asked too many questions. My all-time favourite was, she would claw your eyes out and come back and shit in the sockets if someone wasn't trustworthy. She was the first of our family to get a telephone in her house. We would ring her from the phone box in Fishburn and she would answer, "Sedgefield 276." Funny how that sticks in my head.

Uncle Arnold was a joiner and made lovely furniture in his workshop at the back of the house.

Fishburn was a small village and most people knew each other. Three of the main businesses in the village were owned and run by my mother's aunts and uncles, being my grandmother's brother and sisters. Uncle Harold and Aunty Marie Walton had the Newsagents. Uncle Charles and Aunty Dora McKeen, had the Grocers, and Uncle Douglas and Aunty Margaret Scott had the Post Office. Dora and Margaret were Granny's sisters and Harold her brother. Uncle Harold was my favourite; I was the son he never had. We could go to Uncle Harold's Newsagents and help him sort newspapers and get a back hander off him (money). I would go with him on a morning down to Thorpe Thewles, near Stockton, to pick up the papers. Plus, I used to steal cigarettes from him, five Woodbines and a penny book of matches. I didn't do it that often. He was a great character; he had a dog called Bruno, an Airedale Terrier, who would howl when he played his violin. Uncle Harold and Aunty Marie (pronounced marry), never drank out of their teacups, they would pour the tea into the saucer and drink from that. STRANGE. They would often share the tea in the saucer with the dog. They were very old fashioned and I used to be tickled that they always referred to the kitchen as the scullery! Uncle Harold built his own house, on the Front Street, with the newsagents downstairs, but didn't live there long as he died. I was never allowed to go to the funeral as my mother said it was no place for kids, she couldn't be bothered to get us all ready was more like it.

Aunty Marie sold up and moved to Ferryhill.

Uncle Charles and Aunty Dora lived above the Grocery shop, next to Danby's Farm, and had pictures of 'The Royal Family' on the walls. They were thoroughly nice people and we never swore in front of them. I got caught stealing a penny bubble gum, from his shop, by Uncle Charles and I was so embarrassed. They had two sons who were a lot older than us so we never really had a lot to do with them.

Uncle Douglas was a Justice of the Peace and lived in the Post Office which Aunty Margaret ran. Douglas was a strong silent type who smoked a pipe. I loved the smell. He wore old fashioned 1940s' type suits and had a garden to die for. Greenhouse and every type of flower growing that you could imagine. He would often send bunches of flowers home with me. His wife, Aunty Margaret, I have purposely left until last. If you have ever seen the Giles cartoons, she was the granny. Po faced, old fashioned, never had children, no personality and worse than that, holier than thou! She used to be forever winning the Premium Bonds, going to Eastbourne for holidays every year and she had even been to one of the Queen's Garden Parties. She used to give us a glass of pop when we went there. I can reconstruct the taste to this day by adding orange cordial to lemonade. The smell takes me back to her cold dark austere house behind the Post Office. Madge became Aunty Margaret in later life.

We never knew my father's family, at the time, and they never came into our lives until years later.

So the first five years of my life were spent here at number 5 Maughan Terrace, a small and poky three bed roomed house which fronted onto the main road and it had a back yard. The yard led onto a back lane and a playing field, and beyond that Allotments where the locals grew their vegetables and kept chickens, and once there was a turkey, we were petrified of it. All of the women hung their washing out across the back lane and then scrambled to get it in when the coal man or milk man came with their horse and carts. I loved the smell of the horses. The milk depot was at the end of our street so seeing the horse and carts was a daily occurrence. Our back yard had an outside toilet or "Netty" as my gran used to call it. We played in the street with whatever we could lay our hands on. A Beano Annual and a skate made a great skateboard. I remember I had a scooter. I learned to roller skate and we had communal games like hide and seek. The girls played "two baller" and "skippy". My eldest sister, Christine, was the favourite niece of Aunty Margaret and Uncle Douglas at the Post Office. They were childless so always made a fuss of Christine but never the boys. (Actually, if you saw the miserable face on Aunty Margaret, you would understand why she had no kids.) They gave Christine an old Post Office bike which we used to steal out of our yard and scoot along on it with one foot on a pedal. It was far too big for us but we were good at improvising. After a hard day's play, we were fed and bathed in the kitchen sink. We didn't have a bathroom.

We only had two rooms downstairs, one of which was the Lounge or Sitting Room we called it, and the kitchen. There was a wooden extension at the back of the house which acted as a combined shed, wash house and entrance hall. The front door to the house led straight out onto the main road so that only got used now and again.

Fishburn was a mining village in those days and the whole of life revolved around the pit. My earliest memories were the billowing clouds of stinking steam that used to belch out of the Coke Ovens and envelop the community. I am privileged to remember the stables at the pit head and the Pit Ponies that used to pull the coal tubs underground. I think that my love of horses was born from these encounters. I remember visiting the pit in those days and as there were no restrictions, we could wander freely through the grounds. I got the shock of my life when I poked my head through a door near the clocking off machine, one day, and seeing rows of naked men having a shower. What a shock! Our parents were from the old school and we had to remain covered up at all times. It was drummed into us so thoroughly that I even had nightmares about walking down the street with just my vest on and it was getting shorter and shorter I had to pull it right down at the front so people would not see my willy. Well, the contrast of the stark white, lean hard bodies that never saw sunlight and the black coal dust still remains with me to this day.

At the top end of our street was a cinema (the opposite end to the dairy) where we would go to see Tarzan films. I loved them. I wanted to be Jai the little boy who swings around with Tarzan. Opposite the cinema was Frampton's shop where they sold sweets and just up from Frampton's was the Fish and Chip Shop and Jennie Proud's. another sweet shop. We were enterprising in those days, selling bunches of wild flowers around the doors to get money to go to buy sweets or go to the cinema. Our Cinema eventually closed and got made into a Bingo Hall, so we had to travel to Trimdon Cinema. Mother would give me two bobs (two shillings), that was enough for the bus fare and entrance plus sweets. My favourite film at that time was Atheseus and the Minotaur and this came up in later life, totally by chance.

It was in 5 Maughan Terrace that I tried my first cigarette. Both of my parents smoked and I think most people did in those days. I stole a cigarette and lit it, I nearly choked. It was awful. You would have thought that the experience would put me off for life but it didn't.

Another fond memory of 5, Maughan Terrace was the vicar calling in on a Sunday and being shown into the Sitting Room. We had all been to Sunday School and were lined up along the sofa whilst Mother and the vicar occupied the seats at either side of the fireplace. Now on our mantelpiece above the fireplace we had a set of china dogs and unfortunately, I had been playing with them and had arranged them on each other's backs just as I had seen the dogs in the back street. I nudged my brother and sister to let them know and we had to sit there dying to laugh. I still think it is hilarious to this day.

I remember my first day at school so well, sitting at the back of the class with Stephen Martin who I considered to be my cousin. In those days all of your parents' friends were called aunty and uncle. So Fred and Sylvia Martin, who lived down our street, were always Aunty Sylvia and Uncle Fred. I remember them well; they had a Boxer Dog called Bengo and his muck was all over their back yard. You had to tip toe through it all to get to the back door. Anyway, Steven and I were great pals and our seats at the back of the class allowed me to steal pockets full of furniture from the doll house which was directly behind us. The Martins moved to Stockton and onto Canada but I remember them well.

It was during one of my first days at school that I put my hand up and asked to go to the toilet. The teacher asked me if I knew where it was. Of course I knew, it was "the Netty" in our back yard at home. So off I trotted all the way home for a pee and back again. No one had thought to show us where the school toilets were.

I was 5 years old, and had just started school, when I contacted Anaemia and Glandular Fever and had to go into Hospital halfway between Fishburn and Sedgefield. (It was two and a half miles to Sedgefield.) So I missed about six to eight weeks of my first year at school. I was in the children's ward for weeks and was just about to be released when I contacted Measles so had to stay in. I had some fun in hospital even though I was only five. I remember starting a water fight and getting into trouble from the nurses. People used to come and visit me and bring me sweets and presents. The best present by far was a black and white Police Car with a blue flashing light on the top, I loved it. I could never see the point of the wooden building blocks that someone brought for me.

My Aunty Dorothy worked in the Hospital Kitchen and would come and visit me, which is more than I can say for my parents.

Shortly after leaving hospital I was taken to my grandmother's in Sedgefield to stay and I remember screaming the place down because I didn't want to. I started wetting the bed again and did so until I was 10 or more, years old. I used to get belted off my father for doing it.

We moved from Maughan Terrace shortly after I left hospital, to 52 Moorside Crescent. I never got over the fact that my favourite toy garage with my corgi and dinky cars never made it in the move. It was just around the corner, off the main road and had an enormous garden front and back. We needed a bigger house as there were now 5 children and our parents. This house had a large fireplace with bread ovens in the front room. Dad put up a swing for us in the back garden. The front garden was a lawn to play on, bordered with Orange and Purple Iris'. Across the street was Mrs Wilkes who I used to run messages for and get 3d (three pence) equivalent to 1.5p these days. If I did a few messages I would get 6d (sixpence) which to me was a fortune in those days. I spent every penny on sweets.

The biggest bonus in Moorside Cres was that we had a bathroom. What a luxury, a great big white bath. We were too old to be bathed in the sink by now. The only down side was that it was right next to the kitchen at the back of the house. We still had an outside Netty. There was a cupboard in the bathroom with the hot water tank in it. We discovered some treasure one day behind the tank. A whole box of aircraft pilots' face masks (Dr Whites sanitary wear). They must have been hidden for Christmas (we thought). We quickly put the loops over our ears and proceeded to run around the garden with our arms outstretched playing bomber pilots. Great fun!

We knew all the kids in the street and had seasons for marbles, conkers, roller skating, etc. We would walk the two and a half miles to Sedgefield to get the best conkers (chestnuts). The whole street would come out to play British Bulldog and Cricket across the road. We had very few cars so it was safe to play in the street. I say the whole of the street would come out to play, we had a group of catholic kids who lived at the end of the street near the main road and they never mixed with us. They were really treated like aliens in those days. We had one of them cornered one day and had his life. He was crying as we taunted him that he stank and there was a yellow shitty fly round him. (The ones that you find on cow pats.) How cruel we were!

We would go bird nesting and collecting eggs. We knew all the local birds, Skylarks, Crows, Yellow Hammers, and Bullfinches etc. We had books about their habitat and nesting habits. We knew exactly where to find them and would wander for miles in search of them. Carr's pond was down the road and we would go to see ducks and swans. We were petrified of the swans as someone told us that they could break your arm if they came near to you. It didn't stop us trying to get as close to their nest as possible to see the enormous eggs. We would wander for miles and our mother never worried about where we were. If we were hungry, we would go home or I have sat on a bale of straw in a field and chopped a stolen turnip up with my penknife and eaten it.

We would collect Rosehips when they were in season and sell them for a shilling a pound (weight). My best friend, Alan, and I would sit up in the trees in the orchard, opposite his house, smoking and discussing where to go bird nesting. I would have stolen the five woodbines and a penny book of matches from my Uncle Harold's Newsagents. I wasn't a serial thief but I have been known to help myself from big shops and rich people.

I changed schools and went to the Fishburn Junior Mixed School, there was nothing mixed about it. Yes, there were girls at the school but segregated to the maximum. The Boys

Playground was at the back of the school and the Girls Playground at the front. I had finished at Infants School and although I cannot remember the change over, I was installed in this great big red brick school, and it was a major offence if boys went into the girls' part of the yard or vice versa. There was even a white line painted on the tarmac to divide the two. If we wanted to talk to the girls we had to chat from our side of the line. We developed this game called "Grabs" where we grabbed a feel of the girls' genitals over the line and they did likewise to us boys. It was all harmless fun and an essential part of growing up in a village. I am not sure it would be regarded as such in these ridiculous times. I left Fishburn when I was ten years old so I could only have been about 8 when we played this. Out of school we played "Dirty Hospitals" with the girls, where one of the gang had to be the patient and everyone else had a look or a feel of some forbidden place on the poor unfortunate's body.

The school had a glass veranda running the full length at the back of the classrooms. The Boys' Playground was flanked by trees where we would collect sycamore keys and conkers. The toilets were outside, and had no roof, against the back wall of the Boys Playground. They stank and the urinals got clogged up with Sycamore keys and leaves but no one cleaned them out. I just have to walk into a smelly public toilet these days and I am back in that school toilet. As it was outside away from prying eyes, we boys would have competitions to see who could pee highest up the wall. (That's probably why they stank.)

At the front of the school bordering the girls' playground were fruit trees. I remember the plums distinctly. We were in assembly one morning when Mr Edwards announced that there was only one plum left on the trees at the front and no one was to pick it. So after school I obeyed his instructions to the letter. I stood on the school fence and ate the plum whilst it still hung from the tree. The remains were still hanging there next morning. Of course I never owned up to it.

Again, at school, we had our seasonal games we played. Cops and Robbers, Conkers, Japs and English, Marbles. We made great long icy slides diagonally across the playground in the winter. And the most barbaric game that I cannot remember the name of, where one person stands bending over with their head on a wall and everyone takes a run and jump to try and pile on top of them.

Mr Edwards, the Headmaster would let us put plays and poems on across the school intercom system on a weekly basis. This was one of my absolute favourite spots and I would write poems and dream of performing it on the "speaker in the classroom". I learned to play the recorder at this school and I can still remember the tunes I was taught to this day. Happy memories!

Annual highlights in Fishburn were The Club Trip and Durham Miners Gala. We looked forward to both. A Workingman's Club had been built next to the Playing Field behind Maughan Terrace. They collected funds all year to take us to the seaside. We would have to get up early to get on the bus. We would be handed two bob (two shillings) and a bag of sweets for the journey. We only went to Seaton Carew or Saltburn but what a treat.

On the day of The Durham Miners Gala, our local colliery band would march through Fishburn with their banner and play. I loved the sound of the cornets and the big bass drum. All the village kids would follow along behind them. They

32

eventually got on a bus and went up to Durham to play and listen to a speech by Harold Wilson, the Prime Minister, from the balcony of The County Hotel in Elvet.

It was during this time that I joined the Cubs and we had meetings, down the colliery hut, once a week. We could never afford the uniform but we used to attend and "Akela" would show us how to make fires (as if we didn't already know), make knots etc. My favourite was "Bob a Job week". Where you went out into the community and did jobs for a shilling (a bob). I made a fortune, BUT I wasn't going to hand it into the Cubs. I bought a £1 Premium Bond and spent the rest on sweets.

We had many enterprising ways of making money. If we delivered leaflets around the doors for Uncle Charlie at the Grocers, he would reward us with half a crown (two shillings and sixpence) and a bag of sweets. Or I could go and help Uncle Harold sort papers and get paid. It was whilst helping Uncle Harold one day that my brother Alan came one day to tell me that my pet rabbits had died. I was so upset. I had two lovely white rabbits that I kept in a wooden hutch in the back garden. To this day I don't understand my reaction as my previous white rabbit was skinned and floating in a sink full of water, when I came in from school, ready to go to the butchers along the street, Father had sold it so that he could get a packet of tabs (cigarettes). That never bothered me.

We learned all about sex in Fishburn. We grew up seeing the cows "doing it" in the fields, dogs "doing it" in the street. Someone at school told me how humans had sex and I was adamant that my parents did NOT do such a thing. (Even though they had five kids.) My eldest sister Christine showed me with pelvic thrusts what men did to women, again I wasn't convinced. Then one fateful day we went for a walk down to the Hardwick Park in Sedgefield. We looked over a wall and there in the grass was this couple who could only be described as "hammering away at each other"! I was mortified. I even witnessed the ejaculation. So it was true after all. It must have been quite a while after that we used to go for wanking fun in the garages. I was too young, less than ten, so it wasn't much fun for me, but we used to watch the older boys doing it.

We also learned how to swear. Bloody and Bugga were like God Bless you. Everyone used them. We used to tell each other to Piss off, vulgar I know, but the stark realities of life were never hidden from us. Someone wrote that a certain girl was a Pros (short for prostitute) on the Cubs Hut door. I was still none the wiser when I asked an older boy to explain it to me. We were stuck in this village close to Geordie land and learned all the phrases as well as the Pitmatic language used by the miners. Gan on man! And Shut thee gob! Am gannin yam! I am going home. We also learned when and when not to use it. These days I can cuss and swear in about 5 languages, if there was a degree in it, I would get a Masters. Madge would go ballistic if we didn't talk properly.

The Potts Family, Father's Close Relatives

I never had cause to question Father's side of the family nor wonder if he had any. I think I was too young to know that they may even exist. Our world revolved around the close relatives, who just happened to be from my mother's side. I was about nine years old when I got taken down to Abbey Hulton in Stoke on Trent, to meet Granny (Thursa) Potts and

Granddad Potts (Bill). They lived at 9, Priory Road and had a large garden. Dad's older sister, Joyce, lived just up the road. She had a daughter, Gloria Jean, and a son Keith, albeit to different fathers but they were our new cousins. Gloria, who we call Glo, was a little bit older and as it was the sixties and she was in the height of fashion, she wore the short skirts and tons of thick black mascara. We were in awe of her as she was so trendy. Gloria has never known who her father is and we joke these days that he must have been an Indian Taxi Driver as she goes so dark skinned after half an hour in the sun. Keith on the other hand was my age and blonde. His surname was Ryder and Aunty Joyce was still living with his father when I first met them all. I broke my heart crying when we had to leave my newly discovered family. Gran had given me a massive box of chocolates to eat on the way home. It turned out that Father had abandoned his family after leaving the Fleet Air Arm and hadn't been back for years. He never told us that he had three brothers. Uncle Billy was the eldest boy, then Albert and Frank the twins. I met Albert years later when he got divorced and moved back in with Gran after Granddad had died. I never met Frank. Uncle Billy I met years later at Glo's 50th Birthday party.

Chapter 2

Teenage Years

We moved from Fishburn when I was ten. At that time, they had a school examination called the Eleven Plus. I was dreading it. My school reports were always the same, either top marks in the subjects that I liked or "could do better" in the subjects that I didn't like. It was years later that I realised that I learn at a very fast pace and have to be stimulated to learn otherwise I go to sleep. So in a class of 30 people, if one person asks a question, I turn off and think about something else. I have proved it to myself, I taught myself to speak German, do Sign Language Alphabet and a few basic expressions. I can teach myself anything. Somewhere along the way though school must have done me some good as I have excellent numerate skills, I am brilliant at spelling and grammar and I remember quite a bit of the French they taught us at junior school.

Anyway, Father took a new job at Ridgehouse in Newton Aycliffe and we moved to a four-bedroom house in this lovely fresh new town (NOT!). 97, Oakfield, was a brand-new house, next to a large playing field with football pitch, tennis courts and a Tuck Shop. All of our lifelong friends in Fishburn were left behind and here I was, a village boy in a place full of "Townies". I was placed in Stephenson Way Junior School, in the fourth year. By this time, they had abolished the Eleven Plus, much to my delight. It was hard work trying to fit in with these strange people. We made friends, we got bullied, we fitted in and eventually I got sent to Marlowe Hall Secondary School. I hated it.

It was during the second or third year at Marlowe Hall that I ran into problems. Puberty had set in. I was in a GCSE Class and was doing relatively well but some of the stuck-up bitches in the class were not of the same sense of humour as me. We had fights and arguments. One girl from South Africa called Betty, I hated her guts and she hated mine. I am still not keen on white South Africans. It's something about their "holier than thou" attitude and arrogance. In my eyes we are all put on this earth as equals. Anyway, I was dropped down a grade and was delegated to going to school with the dunces. I lost interest and couldn't wait to leave. Even when we moved across to Woodham Comprehensive School, which had just been built, I used to skive for weeks on end. I would rather go up to the farm and earn a few bobs than go and sit in a classroom.

I had never had a need to fight when I was growing up in Fishburn as the village kids all got on so well. We must have had a few squabbles but never fist fights. So the thought of fighting was quite alien to me. I was in a woodwork class at school when one of the school bullies started on me (Jeff). I took so much and then my temper kicked in. Right you, on the park field after school, I announced. Well, there we were all polite, you hit me first, no you hit me first. So I clobbered the bugga, there was blood everywhere. I quite enjoyed doing it. His mother was screaming from one end of the field and my mother from the other. He never picked on me again. It was during our first year at Newton Aycliffe that I managed to learn to ride a horse. A neighbour had a friend whose daughter had a grey pony called Smoky. I could go and ride it when I wanted. He was a bugga to catch in his small paddock next to Simpasture Shops, close to where I lived. I spent hours chasing him, I got kicked a few times but eventually I would arrange the show jumps into a trap and corner him. Oh bliss, I would put his saddle and bridle on and trot around his paddock. He must have been bored out of his skull but I was in heaven. I eventually met other kids with ponies and through dogged determination, I would cadge rides. On two occasions I stole a £1 from Madge's purse and went up to Dormerstiles Riding School in Heighington, run by Verna Gibbon. I had my lessons on a little fat Shetland pony called Taffy. It was great but Mrs Gibbon talked a new language that I didn't understand. When the pony was having a pee, she called it "spending a penny", stand up in your stirrups, he's spending a penny! I hadn't a clue what she meant. If she said it was having a piss then all well and good. To this day I still ride like an old farmer but we will come to that later.

I think I never really forgot about being a village boy so I never settled into town pursuits. I hated ball games (still do); to me dogs were put on this earth to chase balls. I did try Badminton for a while but again boring. It's the rules that I hate, I like to be free. I had a racing bike so after school I would be down the country lanes, helping on farms and riding horses. I was rapidly becoming a teenager and I started to dance and listen to music. I loved soul music, from 15 years old Aretha Franklin has been my heroine, along with Otis Reading, The Four Tops, and The Supremes etc. I started going to The Methodist Youth Club, 'The Methy', I was good at dancing and loved the music. I would meet my friends and have a great old time. We then hit on the idea to go to the Youth Club in Heighington. The appeal to me, but unbeknown at the time, was that Heighington was a village. We made friends and I enjoyed the nights there.

I started to help the blacksmith at the Dog Inn outside Heighington. I loved going with him to the Zetland Hunt and big posh houses to shoe these magnificent beasts. I would pump the bellows and hold the horses. In turn I used to ride his horses and then one fateful day his niece, Wendy, came down and asked me to go and ride her pony, Scamp, a black fell pony, which she kept up at Redworth about two miles away. I had to cycle there, collect the saddle and bridle from her house in the village and cycle up the lane to where she kept Scamp. I was in heaven; it was almost like having your own pony. I rode for miles around the lanes and through villages. I was coming back down the lane one day on my bike when I was stopped by the farmer at the top of the hill, Dougy Earl. He lived with his wife Doreen and we became firm friends. I never rode Scamp again; Dougy had thoroughbred horses so I stepped up a grade. Mind you he also had a little strawberry roan pony called Tony, he taught me to jump on. I was on a lunge rein in the stack yard, which had a clinker bottom (ash). There were hay bales stood on end so about 2 foot 6 inches high, around I would go, bareback, jumping these enormous hay bales. I could never fall off as the rough clinker bottom would be horrendous. it taught me the rudiments.

At this time, Dougy came back from the sales one day with the most magnificent chestnut thoroughbred stallion called Hardene, we called him Bronze. His coat was like burnished copper. He had caught his eye on the starting post whilst racing and was going blind in it. I had my first ever days Hunting on him. I think I was only about 12 or 13. It was a real buzz riding this massive horse; I used to ride with my stirrups short as if I was racing. Well, whilst I was in my seventh heaven riding Bronze and hunting, Bronze had other ideas. My pal Pat Thompson was on her immaculate grey thoroughbred mare called Jane. I am not sure if Jane was winking at Bronze (horsey folk will understand that), but nature was taking its course. Bronze's fifth leg was unfolding and mating was his game. So a very posh lady told me that perhaps I might want to go for a trot round. What the hell for? I eventually cottoned on and we went for quite a few trot rounds BUT there was one incident when he tried to mount Jane, poor Pat got a puff of hot breath down her neck. It was time for home!

Another notable horse of Doug's was a lovely mare called Fruitika, stable name Queeny, he had bred her himself from his mare Fruitina. She was bright bay with a white blaze. Only about 15.2 hh but had just come out of training with a blood disorder. She was fighting fit. We were having a gallop round an oblong field with Doug's friend Lol on his chestnut hunter. It was so invigorating; I have never been so fast. We stopped for a breather and Doug whispered to me to let Queeny go down the long side of the field heading for home. Just to show Lol that Queeny was a better horse, no doubt. Well, I did it, we went once round and coming onto the long side I let her go, Christ she could cover the ground. At the bottom of the field was a small hedge of about 3-foot high but with a 6-foot drop at the other side, one field from home (the farm)! Queeny was going that fast and would not slow up, I was sure she would not be able to corner at this speed so I sat tight to jump. She jammed the anchors on last minute and slid right up to the hedge. I meanwhile flew through the air but my right foot was jammed in the stirrup, with the stirrup leather across her back. My other foot was at the other side of the hawthorn hedge, not nice. Luckily for me I held onto her bridle. She was fighting to get away and wasn't helped by Doug running down the field shouting and swearing. He soon shut up when he saw my predicament. My jeans were in tatters; my pride was in my boots. I never rode her again.

I was helping Doug one day with hay time, I should have been at school, and we were leading bales and putting them up on the stack in the yard across from his house. I came down off the stack for a drink that Doug's wife, Doreen, had brought for us. To get back up on the stack, I sat on a bale going up the elevator. Halfway up, the bale rolled and I came off, my leg went through the elevator wooden slats and started to strip the skin off my shin. What a mess. Imagine the end of the day, I had to cycle home and tell my mother that I had fallen off my bike. She didn't believe me.

Uncle Douglas' Funeral

During my later teenage years, when I had learned to drive, Uncle Douglas from Fishburn died. We as a family went to the funeral in the small chapel in Fishburn. We walked behind the hearse to the church. Neville was in front of me and I could see his shoulders moving, I thought he was laughing, really he was crying. This was my first funeral so I didn't quite know how to behave. We filed into church and to our surprise, there was Granny Jopling (Etty), sitting in the back pew. We were surprised as she and Aunty Margaret didn't get on. On seeing Etty I turned to my sister, Christine, and said, "I should have put the horse box on, Granny will want a lift home to Sedgefield!" We giggled.

The service went along uneventful and we then went out to the graveside. The biggest farce then ensued that I laughed my head off. The coffin was just about to be lowered into the grave when one of the supporting tapes snapped and the coffin came crashing down onto the hard earth at the side of the grave. The coffin lid came open and we could see Uncle Douglas' head. Aunty Margaret all the while was standing at the grave side, breaking her heart and was oblivious to what had happened, which made it funnier. I had to move away as I was crying laughing.

Years later when Margaret died, my mother and Dorothy were sole beneficiaries. They found money all over the house which was surprising when you take into account that Aunty Margaret used to sit huddled over half a dozen coals burning in the grate whilst wearing two overcoats. I didn't go to her funeral but went to the house with Elaine, my cousin, on the day of the funeral, but after the ceremony. We found all sorts in the bin. Madge and Dorothy had thrown away what they thought was old fashioned rubbish. I got a complete silver cutlery service in a beautiful oak box, a pair of war issue binoculars, six silver teaspoons and sugar tongs in a presentation box, and various other treasures out of the bin! I hid them in the attic at Madge's for years. I showed the cutlery service to Madge about 20 years later at my house in Cleasby and told her where I had got it from. That makes it mine she replied. What a bitch! I went up into the attic as I knew that neither my mother nor Dorothy would have searched there. The only thing there was an old gas mask. Elaine was on the landing and asked what was there. A skeleton I replied as I threw it down at her. She screamed as the head piece looked like a skull and the breathing pipe like a backbone. Well, what the poor neighbours thought we will never know, the day of the funeral and all the laughing and screaming going on in the house.

Chapter 3

An Upsetting Experience

During our teenage years my parents had some friends called Jim and Joyce Barron who lived across town, they socialised together. They had one daughter, Christine who was Carolyn's age. They would socialise with Madge and Roy and they even came on holiday with us a couple of times, we thought of them as aunty and uncle. Jim was a great joker so was very popular with us older kids. Then one day, Jim left Joyce for another woman. I really felt bad for Joyce but doubly so when Madge and Roy dropped her like a stone. They disowned her at her time of need. I thought at the time that it was despicable way to treat a friend and have done ever since. In their tiny minds my mother and father thought of Joyce as a threat. She was single and not to be trusted. I am so glad that I can't even start to be that petty and small minded.

Showdowns

Once I hit teenage years I began to stand up to my father. I wasn't going to put up with his beatings anymore and I would certainly put MY point across. The first showdown occurred when I got my first job and my first paycheque. I asked Father to cash it for me. Think about it folks, first paycheque, what would any normal teenager want to do with it? Blow it all of course! I waited all day for him to come back from work with the money. He came home from work and what had he done, opened up a bank account for me. I went absolutely ballistic. Another 5 working days before I could get my hands on the money, was he stark raving bonkers. I was screaming at him in the dining room and banging things about, Mother was past herself in the kitchen because I was daring to stand up to him, Master of the house, he who must be obeyed. He never retaliated so the argument just fizzled out.

The next showdown occurred when I was packed and ready to go to a farm in Darlington to do my year's practical on a farm, prior to going to Agricultural College. I had been having stomach troubles and had pills to settle it down. Thinking about it now, it was probably the stress of leaving home that made my stomach upset. Now I am the sort of person that if you ask me a stupid question, I will give you a stupid answer. Christine had seen the pills and asked what they were. Drugs, I replied.

Remember this was early '70s' and drugs were very much to the foreground in the press. And why women do this I will never understand, she blabbed it to Father. Remember he was a small-minded Victorian idiot, I got thumped, shouted at and there was no way that these were not drugs, in his mind. What a fight I had with him that day.

My mother was having the old aunts around for a buffet at her house on one occasion, when I was home. We were all invited too. Madge's buffets were extremely predictable, boiled eggs, cheese, coleslaw, ham, salad, quiche, all out of packets, nothing homemade. "Same old, same old." I was asked to help the old dears to get their plates filled as they couldn't reach as well as I could.

Remember readers that they were all dull and boring with not a jot of a sense of humour, just like my mother. I livened up the monotony by asking the old aunts politely, "Would you like some egg?" but I fused the last two words and said Smeg (Cock cheese). None of them would have a clue what it was, especially Madge. My sister and I started laughing, that's a sin in itself in Madge's house. Madge came over and kicked me and told me to behave myself. I still think it's hilarious.

Starting Work

I left School at 15 with no qualifications. I hadn't a clue what I wanted to do in life. I stacked shelves in Fine Fare Supermarket for a while and got the sack because the Manager thought that I was pilfering when in fact it had been the evening shelf stackers doing it. I am the first to admit if I have done something wrong but try and convince your father and the shop manager that. There was a nice lad Steve who got the boot at the same time as me for the same reason.

I then went into a Gents' outfitters called Hackett and Baines run by a lovely family from Shildon called Tarry. Philip the son was running the Newton Aycliffe Branch, he was charming and extremely motivating. I got on a treat and loved it. By this time my ex school friend, Angus, had changed his name to Benny and he convinced me to use my middle name, Roy. So at work I was known as Roy. It was great to have a weekly wage. I had started smoking, thanks to Angus, and I had started going to Sam Hall's Racing Stable, Spigot Lodge, Wensley, on a weekend to visit another school friend, Evvie, who was an apprentice jockey. I would get the bus and spend the day there. It was fantastic. Working with famous race horses whose names were constantly on the TV. Tamerlane and Roebuck spring to mind. Paddy the Head Lad was a force to be reckoned with. I loved horses but had decided that they were to be a hobby and not a career. I never wanted to get sick of them and I certainly never wanted to be a horsey bore.

Chapter 4

The Start of My Career

I eventually decided that I was going into farming. Horses and farming went hand in hand in my mind. You couldn't have one without the other. I did my year's practical experience in Darlington, Snipe House Farm, run by Joe (son) and George (father) Richardson. They had a small herd of twenty Friesian cows which I milked but better still they had race horses. So I got to ride again and didn't learn a great deal about farming. I was hardly inspired to, looking back, I only got £4 a week and my board and keep. Half a day off a week, Sunday afternoon, to go home. Sounds like a Catherine Cookson novel doesn't it?

I got to Durham Agricultural College in 1971 aged 17 going on 18 and spent 2 years there. I was going to be taken to college by Father but at the last minute a white transit van arrived at home, driven by one of his men, to take me. I failed the first year and had to sit a re-entrance exam to get back for the second year. I achieved an A.N.C.A. (Advanced National Certificate in Agriculture), and being me, I have to be busy, I also did a Horse Course and Soil Analysis and Testing course in my second year. The soil testing was in preparation for a job that the lecturer had lined up for me on leaving. My dissertation was on maximising potato production which I found fascinating, NOT!!

The social life at college was brilliant, we spent our free time at Nevilles Cross Teacher Training College going to discos and the bar. We had more friends there than at our own college. I really don't know how I managed, I had very little money. My grant went nowhere. My parental contribution never manifested itself. I had to cycle 11 miles to The Eden Arms Hotel at Rushyford, close to home, to wash glasses in the cocktail bar on a Saturday night, to get a few pounds to see me through the next week. Why I smoked I do not know! I tried a couple of times to give up and never succeeded.

During my second year at Houghall I asked the principal for special permission to keep a horse in one of the paddocks close to my accommodation. I got the OK. I was the first person to ever take a horse to Houghall. What an honour. Robin the horse didn't think it an honour. He was a pig from the word go. I couldn't catch him. On the few occasions I did catch him we had lovely rides along the river in Durham, down to Shincliffe, round Houghall Farm. Then one day I went to catch him and he jumped into the next paddock, and the next one and the next one, all seven of them in fact. Galloped over the brand-new cricket crease. I was furious but gave chase. He went all the way down to the farm where I almost got a hold of him, then he headed for Shincliffe, galloped all around the vicar's garden and lawn, what a mess! I was livid. I eventually caught him in Sherburn, miles away. The little shit! I got him back to Houghall and saddled him up and rode him home to Carrsides. All eleven miles of it. To add insult to injury, I got just to the top of the farm lane and Ralph was in the yard playing with a football. He banged it off the garage door and Robin spooked and I fell off. So readers, Robin went down the road!

A major incident happened at Houghall. I had a girlfriend called Gillian, she was a senior at one of the top girls' schools in Durham. I had been informed that my cousin Paula was riding at the Wensleydale Show so I got it into my head that I would go to watch. Gillian decided that she would come with me. I never asked her to. Neither of us had any money so we had to hitch hike the 25–30 miles. It was a bit like hard work but we got to Downholme which was only about seven miles from the show, and she started. She was sick of this, wanted to go home, she didn't want to see me again. I think the feeling was mutual. So I never got to the show but I vowed that I would never ever again allow a woman to mess up what I set out to achieve, and that stands even today.

On leaving college, I can't exactly remember the circumstances, but Father could not come and pick me up. I had to hitch hike down the motorway with all my possessions, suitcases, record player etc. I managed to get to the Aycliffe junction on the motorway and started walking. I walked about two miles before I sat down and cried. I just could not go on any further. I had no money. I think I must have got a lift the rest of the way but imagine my surprise when I walked in the house and there was Mother and Father sitting watching TV. That was typical, they never put themselves out for us. They knew it was my final day but not a word or offer to come and pick me up. Selfish all the way!

One weekend we got wind of a Young Farmers Dance at Carrsides Farm, Rushyford. So I went with Sheila Wright who was at college with me. We had a great night and I was introduced to Keith Wilkinson who lived at Carrsides. We became firm friends and I started milking there on a weekend which helped me through college. I went to work at Carrsides after I left Houghall and stayed a number of years. Mrs Wilkinson (Keith's mother) became like a second mother to me, she fed me and looked after me. She was everything that my mother wasn't. I didn't know that at the time. She always taught us that what you give out you get back. A motto that I abide by to this day. Doreen Wilkinson was there for her children through thick and thin. I remember she broke her heart when Ruth left home even though Ruth was in her late twenties.

I started to knock around with Keith's younger brother Ralph, there was only 6 months in age between us and we had more or less the same sense of humour. Sack Barrow races in the feed store was one of our specialities, much to his dad's disgust. We hated Thursdays as we had to muck out 5 thousand battery hens. Ralph used to call the shit "marmalade". It came off the conveyor belts and splashed everywhere. It got in your hair, your eyes and your mouth. Sloppy hen shit liberally strewn with feathers and broken eggs. There was nothing worse, and all so that Joe Public could have cheap eggs.

Ralph and I had a weekly rota for a social life. Saturdays was at A66 Motel. Sunday lunchtime was Stanwick Arms at Aldbrough St John and Sunday night Eden Arms at Rushyford. Tuesday was Grab a Granny at Hardwick Hall. Then there was the usual array of Young Farmers Dances, 21st's and other parties. I had got myself a horse by now and started hunting with the South Durham. Supermoss was a Dark Bay thoroughbred stallion. I called him Moss. He would scream like an idiot when he saw other horses. He was such a handful that I didn't keep him long. I think that after him I got Castle Hill, he was a trotter but had been too heavily handicapped that he couldn't race in this country. I hunted him for two or three seasons. He was brilliant for road work as he could trot at a mile in three minutes. He was bolshie and had no mouth, the harder you pulled, the harder he went. That was pretty frightening. I was on him one day when the hounds met at Hurwoth Burn, near Trimdon. My best pal Shirley worked as a groom at the Hunt Kennels and we rode round together. At the meet we heard a horse squeal but thought nothing of it. Anyway, we got going and went full tilt across about four fields. It's hard work galloping even though the horse is doing all the work. We stopped to get our breath and Shirley sidled up to me and said, "Don't look now but Roger… is crying." I nearly wet myself, she did too. Roger is such a drip and as soft as shit. Without a glance back she rode across to him and said in a very concerned manner, having been crying laughing moments before, "Roger, what's the matter?"

"I think I've broken my leg," he replied. Well, I was off my horse and hopping on one leg peeing myself. The soppy bugga had been kicked at the meet. That was what the horse squealing was. Instead of shouting up, he had galloped across four fields on a broken leg.

Castle Hill was black in the summer and dark bay in the winter but had a large white star on his forehead. I decided he was boring so having seen a friend's horse with a lovely white stripe in his tail, I went to Boots the Chemist to get a Hair Colour. I did the most fantastic broad white stripe down his tail. It was platinum blonde. I loved it… but only for about two days. It went yellow with stable stains and try as I might I could not get it back to white, so I had to cut it out.

Castle Hill was a gelding but had been castrated late in life, when he was six, so he had a lot of stallion characteristics. He had rather strong urine and the ammonia in the air some mornings was acrid. It brought tears to your eyes. Plus, his willy was always stinky and cheesy. I asked the vet what could I do and he recommended Epsom Salts in his water once a week and I had to wash his willy gently with a soapy sponge about every fortnight. The problem was that Castle Hill would get an erection whilst I was doing it. So there I was one day in the stable, gently sponging two and a half foot of erect black cock when Doreen Wilkinson's head appeared above the stable door to tell me that my coffee was ready. God I was embarrassed as I let go of this rather large soapy willy. She looked shocked too but it was never mentioned. I am sure she thought it was a bad dream.

I had a bad accident on Castle Hill. He had lost a shoe and the blacksmith could not make it before Saturday, hunting day. So I put it on myself, I had worked with Keith Jackson for long enough in my youth shoeing horses so I knew what to do. Anyway, the hounds met at Great Stainton and off we went. After about two hours the shoe came off so I started to hack home. I hadn't gone far when three horses came trotting up behind me. Hounds are just over here they said, come on have another hour. I relented and we cantered up Cock Lane to see where they were. I was on the right-hand side of the road on a broad grass verge, trying to save Castle Hill's shoeless hoof, when we came up to a pair of deep tractor ruts in the grass leading to a gateway. Castle Hill jumped the first rut but his front legs went down the second one and we went

53

arse over tit. He got up and galloped off and I stood up and realised I was bleeding. I never ever carry alcohol on a horse, BUT I had got a glass hip flask off Mother Wilkinson for Christmas. I pulled my shirt up and there was a 2-inch slash down the side of my belly. Julia who was sitting on her horse fainted off it when she saw it. Someone brought Castle Hill back and he had gashed his knee. I had to tie my stock around it to stem the flow of blood. I was crying, I hadn't meant to hurt him. I got whisked off to the nearest house, the vicarage in Great Stainton where they sat me on the wooden kitchen table and applied "neat TCP" to my open wound. "Christ all f-f-f... bloody mighty!" I screamed. Hardly language for the village vicarage!

I got a lift back to Carrsides with Castle Hill and got the vet straight away, he gave him an anti-tetanus and told me that he would be ok. I was too shaken to drive so I phoned to ask Father to come and pick me up. What a mistake! I got thumped in front of Mr Wilkinson and the Vet for hurting the horse. He drove me home in silence and never once asked me if I was ok. I got changed quickly and took myself off to hospital to get my wound dressed. Neville was in the bedroom when I was getting changed. He nearly fainted when he saw the wound. It was large enough to see the intestines inside. To summarise, I had learned the lesson the hard way, if you make a decision in life, stick to it! The 3 girls who came up and persuaded me to carry on for half an hour, swayed my decision and look what happened.

Castle Hill eventually went across to Ireland to race again, it broke my heart when he went. I really hope he had a good life over there.

The George Hotel Pierce Bridge

This was the MECCA in our area and was a great place to meet on a weekend as well as through the week. You could go in the George any night and meet people that you knew. I started going when Ralph Wilkinson from the farm bought the place along with his business partner Ray Wade. I would help out behind the bars and eventually had a regular part time job, as well as my main job. In fact, I had two jobs, two horses and even two cars at one point. Having gone through Young Farmers with Ralph and his brother Keith, we knew most of the farmers and their sons and daughters in the area. By area we are talking of about 30 square miles, and we all congregated there. Another interesting fact is that my mother's eldest brother, Gordon, had been a regular at the George 20 years before me. He, like me had gone to Houghall Agricultural College, and I think the family thought that I was to follow in his footsteps.

The George stands on the river Tees and is a sprawling old-fashioned coaching inn. If you have ever heard the song about the "Grandfather Clock was too big for the shelf so it stood 90 years in the hall". Well, that is where it stands, in the hall at the George. Another claim to fame from the George is that Dick Turpin is reputed to have hidden in one of the cupboards in the Raby Bar.

Well, having left college and started work and being 18/19 years old, the party time had arrived. We had some grand old affairs there. Parties in the ballroom, "Come as you go to bed" party where you came in your pyjamas and nighties. Tarts & Vicars. We just invited everyone as we were all just one big happy family. Then there were Young Farmers Dances, Hunt Balls, 21st s, Weddings, Farmers Balls. We were never away from the place. Even if we didn't know who was having the party, we would gate crash after the upstairs bars closed. I can't tell you how many times I have had to stay the night as I was too drunk to drive home or it was far too late to drive home (IE 3 or 4 am).

I had been to my first ever Ball at the George shortly after I had left school. The National Hunt Jockeys Ball. My old school friend Evvie Knowles (Everard. He was Ever hard and I was How hard) was riding for Sam Hall at the time and got the tickets. Well, we went, all decked up to the nines in our Dinner Jackets. There were about 20 people to a table and the place was full. Me being me, replaced Evvie's meal ticket in his top pocket for a condom. The waitress on our table came round collecting the tickets and Evvie, without a glance, whipped out his ticket from his top pocket. The waitress without skipping a beat said to him, "Your ticket sir, not your money." Well, I was howling laughing at his very red face. He promised that one day he would pay me back but never did.

Bobby Thompson, the Geordie comedian appeared there one night. He was right up my street. Old fashioned Geordie humour. Sometimes there would be a good soul disco on. I loved soul music. Even if there was nothing on it was great fun just mingling in the bars upstairs. We were all from a farming and horsey background.

I worked at British Steel in Aycliffe for a while as a wages clerk, thoroughly boring! Here I was ensconced in an industry that held no interest to me, working with a set of thoroughly boring people whose only pleasure in life was to finish work and go to the workingmen's club and slosh pints of beer down their dull boring gobs. My job was to balance wages books, rows upon rows of figures. I wasn't allowed to use a calculator. It became second nature that I could tot up figures and it came in handy years later whilst working in bars. I worked in an office with Don, the transport manager, his brother-in-law Bob, who was my boss, and Nigel the train spotter who was roughly about my age but nowhere near the intellect. He spent his time watching trains and courting Joan the receptionist. They had no concept of my country background and my horses and I had no concept of their dull pointless lives. Bob, my boss dropped dead the day after he retired, well there wasn't any point in going on was there? One day a lovely Geordie lady called Frances started in our office. She was like a ray of sunshine. Brilliant sense of humour, but we used to get into trouble for laughing.

It was during my time there, and my mind does not allow me to be exact about the date, sometime in 1977, that Father decided to walk out on our family. It was Christmas Eve. Yes, Christmas Eve! I had gone down to Leicester, with a couple of friends, for a day's hunting with the Basset Hounds, the only pack in the country. We had a great day but I got back home to an empty house. Strange I thought, no one home, Christmas Eve. I went upstairs and there was Carolyn crying in the bed. She was 15. She told me that Father had gone to spend Christmas with his new girlfriend. I was gobsmacked! In fact, what he had done was picked Mother up from work at the Post Office and brought her home for lunch and told her that he didn't want to be a granddad, Christine's daughter, Janine was two years old at the time, took her back to work, and when she had returned at the end of the day he had gone. He had filled the drinks cabinet for us though. That was it, I never saw him again. There had been a court case to get maintenance payments for Carolyn who was still at school, and he had returned to get some more clothes at some point when Mother had smashed a large ceramic ashtray through the rear window of his beloved car. It takes a BIG MAN to walk out on a wife and five kids on Christmas Eve.

I tell a lie, I did see him again, once. I had taken Mother down to Hull where he was living, she had heard that he was in hospital. She went up to see him in the ward, I stayed in the car down in the car park. I didn't want to go as I didn't know how to react to him. I eventually went up and had a few words with him and remember him being exuberant in his show of being glad to see me. He was always full of top show anyway. That was the last I ever saw of him. He died about 20 years later, he was only 60. My brother Alan rang me and told me that he was in Hospital with cancer. It had been too long, I said that I didn't know the man, you may well have rung me and told me that Fred Bloggs from Southampton was dying. Alan had got back in touch with Father when his son Jamie was born. He and his wife wanted Jamie to have two grandfathers. Alan also informed me at some time or other that Father had phoned him to tell him that we had a baby sister. What was wrong with this man? He ran off with another woman, never attempted to keep in touch with us, was arrogant enough to think that we should get in touch with him, and then announces that we have a baby sister. WTF! If Father hadn't run off in such a cowardly way, we may well have afforded him some respect and kept in touch.

My sister Christine idolised my father and she cracked up after he went, even though she didn't live at home. She was married to Keith by this time and had a daughter Janine. She has always been highly strung and tried twice to commit suicide and ended up in the Psychiatric Unit of Darlington Memorial Hospital, Ward P1. She split up with Keith shortly after Father's departure so was that as a result of Father's departure too? Let's not go down that route!

Imagine the faces in our office when I went to the South of France for a two-week holiday and came home with a black suntan. My friend Ian and I had driven down in his brand new, white, TR7 and spend a very enjoyable holiday in Cavalair sur Mer on Camping Croix do Mouton. This is where I met my Dutch friends, they were in the next tent. Ton and I remain friends to this day. Jan, Ton and Felix had driven down from Holland, just as we had from England. So the five of us went around together and down the beach etc. Jan was 6 foot 6 inches and Ton was a big brawny lad. I am telling you this because they came over to England to stay with us for a week. Mother had gone away with Ken for the week (YES, Mother had latched onto the first man that would have her after Father left). I had to cater for them. I didn't know how to cook. They survived anyway but the best night we had with them was at the top Newcastle nightclub, Tuxedo Junction. They didn't understand the dress restrictions as Holland did not have such petty rules. Anyway, we had to find trousers to fit them as they had only brought jeans. I am five foot eleven and the tallest in our family, so six-foot-six Jan borrowed a pair of my trousers. Of course they were half-mast but we told him that it was the fashion. He looked like a clown but we got in no problem. It was a bit of a culture shock for Newcastle as these Dutch lads got up and danced on their own. They didn't need a partner. I can still see Jan in his clown trousers bopping away on his own, on an empty dance floor. What a hoot!

This holiday was my first introduction to a nudist beach. St Tropez was world famous, Pampalone Beach. We went twice but we didn't strip off and quite honestly after an hour we were bored. You start looking for unusual shapes after a while just to ease the monotony. You start off up the beach and people are clothed, then further up topless and then even further, naked. It was a bit of a shock after the Victorian upbringing I had had, but I am open minded and off I went.

The highlight in this dull/sad part of my life was the arrival of Regan (pronounced Raygan) after the little girl in the film, The Exorcist, which was my favourite film at the time, as it was so shocking. She was a 15.2 hands thoroughbred mare and she arrived at Carrsides Farm, lean and scrawny, with a matted winter coat that was dull chestnut with the odd fleck of white hair, and lumpy as she was covered in rain scald. She wasn't a very nice person and was used to having her own way. She was full sister to a horse called Remraf (Farmer backwards), who had won 14 races in a row and had broken his leg so had to be shot. Aunty Vera Crags who bred both of them let me have her on the basis that she never raced and I didn't breed from her. Regan was unbroken so she went away to be broken in. I really had doubts that I was ever going to get on with this horse. She hated kids. All the time I had her she would lay her ears back flat against her head if she got near any. I don't know if she had been mistreated, I doubt it, as she was brought up miles from civilisation. Anyway, I knew when the cowman's kids were close if I was brushing her in the stable because she would bristle and her ears would go back.

A few weeks later I got the phone call that she was broken so I went, with a friend, Janet, to pick her up. I didn't think it was the same horse, even as she stood in the stable, her winter coat had changed to her summer sheen, but still this placid horse, that loaded straight into the trailer couldn't possibly be Regan. We took her back to Carrsides and tacked her up. I told Janet to lead her round and I would lie across her back. I expected ructions but she was as quiet as a mouse. I just could not believe the transformation. I got astride her and she handled like a dream (sounds like a car doesn't it?).

My bond with Regan was brilliant. She got to know what I expected of her and she excelled in everything I tried with her. She was a character and a half. More like a dog than a horse. I hardly ever tied her up. I would put her feed in the manger and shout her from the field, open the gate and she would saunter in. If I was mucking her out, she would follow me across the yard pushing me in the back as I wheeled the barrow. When we got back to the stable, she had to be in before the barrow. She had another trait that I thought was extremely novel. If I was riding out with other horses and I wanted to stop and let the other horses go on, she would go down at the front and scrat like a dog with her two front feet. It was hilarious to see. She was a right little madam. I loved her! There is a saying in the horse world about buying horses with white socks, "One white sock – buy it. Two white socks – try it. Three white socks – doubt it. Four white socks – do without it!" Regan had four white socks and I never ever had reason to doubt her.

The little cow kicked a hound on her first day out hunting with the South Durham. I think it was just too much for her to bear having all these dogs milling around her heels. I was on her back and the yelp told me exactly what she had done. I never taught Regan to jump, she knew all along and was a natural at it. She would ping over anything. She jumped a gate from a standstill one day because I was taking too long in opening the catch. From that day on I had to anticipate what she would do next as she knew only fine well what her job was. We jumped out of a field one day, onto a road, over a quite large post and rails fence. I was so elated that she was jumping it that I forgot to anticipate which direction the hounds were going. Regan hit the ground running and shot off left after the hounds. I shot off right and hit the tarmac with a thud. No bones broken though so back on and on with the job. Regan loved hunting and would show off by sticking her tail in the air like a flue brush, arch her neck and do a bouncy trot whilst lifting her legs in a very pronounced way. A bit like dressage. Her ears would be forward and she would be simply bristling with excitement. A great pleasure to ride as she loved her job!

Fox Hunting

I feel that I should have a quick word about hunting, there are folk who are for it and some folk who are against it. I am neither. There are pros and cons in everything and I make my decisions on calculated assessments from both sides. I did hunt for a number of seasons and with a vengeance for a few seasons when a fox killed all twelve of my hens and three cockerels in the orchard at the farm. The way I see it is that foxes are vermin. You don't hear anyone having an outcry to protect mice and rats caught in traps. The bigger picture is that a lot of farmers wouldn't tolerate foxes on their land if it wasn't for hunting. They would all be gassed. Hunting keeps down the number of foxes to a manageable number, it doesn't exterminate them all.

Farmers keep their animals in factory conditions to keep costs down. So animals living up to their knees in shit all their lives, and chickens in battery cages and veal calves in tiny little pens, in my mind should have more consideration than the odd fox that gets killed. I am more determined to be an ambassador for animals rights these days when dairy farms are like concentration camps for cows, pigs never see the light of day, beef and calves are penned up in dark, musty, damp pens in the heat of summer. And the worst ever scenario is day old calves slaughtered because they are the wrong sex for a dairy herd and the wrong breed to be beef stock. Man-made rules, or man-made stupidity? You decide!

A townie friend of mine announced recently that she had seen a fox outside her house in London and she was going to be anti-blood sports from now on as it was such a beautiful creature. She soon changed he mind when I said, "And how would you feel about it if it had just ripped your cat's throat out?" I think the main issue is YOU are far more guilty about animal cruelty if you live in a town and oblivious to the facts.

You need to go to an abattoir and see the wholesale slaughter of animals to put it all into perspective. I have worked on farms and seen calves de horned without an anaesthetic, to cut costs. I have seen cows get their fully grown horns sawn off, again without an anaesthetic. It's a cruel world at the hands of humans and you protesters should look at your own cruelty too. Let those without guilt cast the first stone! Dogs locked in houses all day without a break. When I was working abroad and living amongst foreign families who I could not communicate with properly, believe me the loneliness was immense. Now apply that to your poor unfortunate pet, your dog, your pony, your goldfish, living a life of solitude because you can only afford one. Don't you think that your pet has rights to a natural life, amongst its own kind so that it can interact and breed and give vent to its natural instincts? It irritates the shit out of me when I see people walking dogs on leads and I know that the poor bugga would rather be running around and venting its pent-up frustrations after being locked up in a house all day. There are far bigger issues to be tackled than the fox hunting debate so save your breath.

I wrote a poem that should sum up my thoughts entirely.

Town Life

You've made a society all of your own, with horrible plastic people,
Their shallow lives all awash, not knowing good from evil,
It's alright to live in a town with your head up in the sky,
Reality a million miles away, and you never have to ask why,
You can breed and fit in with society's plan, buy a house and work in the same street,
Beyond your realm of a few square miles, you blend in with the deceit.
There used to be integrity in every walk of life, but now a throwaway society,
Mingles greed with stress and strife.
You never have to kill your own dinner, it comes in a plastic bag,
Coloured and cut to your own taste because the reality would be a snag.

What you see in the farmyard and out in the fields so green,

Couldn't possibly end up on your dinner plate, now that would be obscene.

Animals are fluffy furry things that you cuddle up in your bed,

Not walking, breathing foodstuff that you have to shoot in the head.

You keep your animals in cages, castrated to suit your needs,

Lavished with love and affection, cos how your poor heart bleeds.

Your dog would rip a lamb's throat out, more so because it is kept,

In unnatural surroundings with its instincts rather inept.

You lock them in your house all day, whilst you are out at work,

No toilet break or contact for the poor little berk.

In the country we treat our animals with the respect that they deserve,

Fellow animals with feelings on this god forsaken earth.

Natural instincts are given consideration, freedom to move about,

As natural a life as they deserve is better without a doubt.

It does contradict slightly what I have just said but I think it quantifies the reality of what is going on. In brief I am saying that when you stop the child molesting and the raping and robbing of old people, that is rife in towns (town sports), then you can come out to the country and tidy up our act.

I had great fun hunting and made some lifelong friends. It's a classless society when you are sitting on a horse in the countryside and I have sat talking to moneyed Lords and Ladies, they all shit in the same pot as far as I am concerned.

I was out hunting with the Zetland Hunt one day when Princess Anne arrived. She was, and still is, I hope, as down to earth as anyone. A few people were bowing and scraping but to me they were overdoing it. All you had to do was be polite. Well, at one point in the day we were trotting in single file down a road when the woman's horse in front of me, let off a string of extremely loud farts. Horses are masters of the art of farting. Well, this daft bugga spun round in her saddle and said, "Oh, I do beg your pardon on his behalf." She was apologising for the horse just because the princess was out. I cried laughing. I bet Princess Anne can fart along with the rest of us!

I have many fond memories of hunting, there is nothing, and I mean NOTHING can compare with galloping across country when your horse is having the time of his life and you are too, jumping whatever you are faced with, even if it was the butcher's garden fence that you just sailed over. Sorry Mr Jewitt from Spennymoor. I hunted mainly with the South Durham Hunt from Sedgefield and then Cub Hunted with the Zetland and later on The West Cumberland Farmers. My social life was second to none. We had Barn Dances, Hunt Balls, National Hunt Jockeys Balls, and BBQs and then there were the 21st Birthday Parties and Young Farmers Parties. There was always something to look forward to. The result of all this social life meant that I knew almost every farmer from North Yorkshire up to Tyneside.

My best friend at that time, and still is to this day, is Shirley Smith. She worked at the hunt kennels for the South Durham Hunt. She could reduce me to tears of laughter with just one look. We both have exactly the same sense of humour, more than slightly skew whiff. Many is the time I have had to get off my horse to cross my legs as I have been peeing myself laughing at something Shirley has said or done. Or I will admit, something she has encouraged me to do, just for a laugh. One that springs to mind, is standing on my horse's back to do an impersonation of someone dancing. Unfortunately, the Huntsman came round the corner and caught me doing it so I got sent home. I still laughed though!

Shirley had this idea that she would start a cottage industry and started collecting hoofs and tails off dead horses. The hoofs were to make ashtrays but what she thought she would do with the tails god only knows. She had them hanging off the garden fence at her cottage at the kennels.

The garden fence! There lies another story. My pal Andy Wood and I were at the kennels one night in Shirley's cottage, sat up chatting all night to her and her house mate Gail. We talked well into the night and the fire was on but none of us dared to go round to the coalhouse to get more coal as there were rats. So we pulled the railings off the garden fence, all six foot of them. There was no way of chopping them up so we put one end in the fire and when that burned away, we kicked another foot into the fire. Ingenious eh?

One sad day, I left my car and horse box at the kennels and hacked my horse over to West Close where the hounds were meeting. I arrived at the farm lane just in time to see a horse box pulling off to the side of the lane to let an oncoming car past. Now I will not go into why a car was coming down the farm lane when hordes of cars and horse boxes were arriving for the Meet. I will just say, guess what sex she was? Well, the horsebox went too far over and the wheel went into a ditch. I watched in horror as the whole horsebox came over and fell onto its side. The last thing I saw was a chestnut horse's leg come crashing out of the window and break under the weight of the box. I felt sick! I couldn't bear to watch so I went past and on up to the meet. Needless to say, I went home early. I put my horse, Castle Hill, in his trailer and went in to see Shirley. We chatted about the accident and she told me that Frank the Kennel man was skinning the horse as we spoke. That night I went to have supper with Shirley. She had cooked some venison which was OK but she admitted later on that it was the horse that had been killed that morning.

Chapter 5

Life at Home

Getting back to Regan. At home I could ride out down the lane and along the main road but on my return, I would come back crashing through the wood at the end of the lane, jump the post and rails into the lane side field, swing round in a circle and jump back onto the lane over a four-foot hedge. I would gallop up the left-hand side of the lane and swing across it and jump the rails into the cow pasture, over the field and jump the low hedge with a big drop into the yard. It was so exhilarating. Regan loved it. There isn't a better feeling in the world than having fun with your horse and knowing that the horse is enjoying every minute of it too!

In the winter when the roads were icy, I would take Regan to Seaton Carew, near Hartlepool, to exercise on the beach. The beach was long and wide with beautiful sand. The only thing spoiling it was a sewer pipe running down the middle of it. I was there one day and a friend of mine, Jane, was there with her Point-to-Point horses. So we decided to have a race. Jane was on her best Pointer, Freddy, and we set off up the beach, full tilt. Regan left them standing and won hands down. I was over the moon with her, but it put Jane's nose out of joint a little bit.

Regan met her demise during my first summer in Spain and here I am thirty years later and I still get extremely emotional when I think about her. Prior to getting Regan I had a little black horse called Pop-on, named after a friend's trotting horse, but really he should have been called Pop Off. He could drop his shoulder, when I least expected it and I would go sprawling on the ground. I can't tell you how many times he did it. Average of about 2 to 3 times a day. I got fed up of him doing it and he went down the road, as they say.

I came home from Newcastle one night in September 1979, the 29th to be precise, to find a police car parked at our door. By this time my mother was having an affair with Ken Smith down the road. I went into our house to find nobody there but looked across the green to Ken's house to see lights on. It was about 2am, so I phoned and a policeman answered the phone. I was asked to go across and found two policemen and Mother and Ken when I got there. There had been a car accident, I was told, and Neville was in Darlington Memorial Hospital. I couldn't take it in. He had been out drinking with his best pal from school, John, and another friend; somehow, they had hit the kerb on Winston Bridge and rolled the car, on the way back from The Four Alls pub in Ovington. The other two got out with bruises but Neville was in the back and got thrown about. I asked, "Shouldn't one of us be there with him?" and the policeman told me that it was too late. To this day I am not sure how it came about, but I had to go and identify him. The euphoria of having been in Newcastle with Joe earlier and now I was sitting in the back of the police car going to Darlington to identify my brother. Neville. He had just had his 21st birthday in March. To anyone who has had to perform this task, my heart goes out to you. I could not believe that the piece of mangled meat on the table when the curtains went back was my little brother, yet the face told me it was. I affirmed that it was him. All the way back to Aycliffe in the police car I felt numb and most of all thought that the task I had just performed should not have been my job. He had died of brain damage. Had he lived he would, no doubt, have been in a wheelchair.

It took me 27 years and a six-year stint in therapy to be able to talk about this.

Something within your being protects you from the enormity of what has happened to you. After the funeral it all got locked inside and although not forgotten about, my mind would not allow me to go there. I couldn't think about it nor talk about it. It was in a hidden vault in the back of my brain. A valid point of note is that I remember being irritated to the back teeth with my mother's outward show of grief at the funeral. She could have got an Oscar for her performance but I felt it was all for show. She insisted on being propped up by her two remaining sons, myself and Alan, she was wringing her hands with ours and did this stumbling walk. The rest of us bore our grief with dignity.

So that was family life as we knew it, over and done! Father had gone, Neville was killed, and Mother went off with Ken Smith. It was 1977 when Father left us and 1979 when Neville was killed. Too many changes, in too short a time. It was as if someone pulled the rug on family life as we knew it!

Newcastle

It was 1978 and I was 23 and I was bored with my social life so I started to go to Newcastle. The nightlife was second to none. I already had friends there that I knew from college but it didn't take long to make more. I met Joe, a solicitor, in a club on Westgate Road and started to knock around with him and his friends. As I sit here typing this, I realise that Joe used to inflict me with mental torture which I didn't know how to deal with. This city life was all foreign to me, and exciting. I enjoyed the freedom and the lack of restraints and morals. I realised that I had been brought up in a very old-fashioned way and looking back now I cherish the morals and integrity far more than the total disrespect for people's feelings and property. I met gays, lesbians, cross dressing men and transvestites, bisexuals. It was like a circus compared to the old-fashioned way that I had been brought up. Joe had a girlfriend, Catherine, and a boyfriend, Jimmy. He played one off against the other and I am ashamed to admit it but I got embroiled as well.

I have never been comfortable with admitting that I am gay and when comparing myself with other gays I prefer to be just me. I don't fit into the category, I am not a stereotypical gay. Just a man who happens to fancy men. And I don't fancy men who think that they are women. I don't mind laughing at camp but cringe when confronted with camp men. In my book, men should be men and women should be women. To this day I can't stand over assertive women nor wimpy girly girls and I want to physically disfigure bitchy men who are bigger bitches than women are. My best friend Penny is a farmer's daughter and is feminine and pretty but drives a wagon and tractors, doesn't mind getting a shovel in her hand. That's how it should be. On the other hand, a good friend of mine has a five-year-old daughter whose mother puts more emphasis on getting false eyelashes and spray tans than feeding her child. She also smokes both cigarettes and dope and all on a very low income. Where is the world going? She reads Hello Magazine and truly believes that that is her life.

What chance does her daughter have? Thank God her father takes charge and looks after her.

So when the big crunch came with our family splitting up, I chose to move to Newcastle with my new interesting friends. What a disaster. I had no job, hadn't the first idea what I would do in Newcastle as I had no experience in a city. It was a downhill roller coaster ride to disaster right from the start. I moved into Joe's house as his second lodger, the other being Martyn. I eventually started to paint the house for Joe as a means of paying rent. It was made so difficult by Joe insisting on me doing four brush strokes from left to right and four strokes up and down to make sure that the paint gets into the grain of the wood. Joe had kicked Jimmy out and this was him going off the rails. I had arrived in Newcastle with two horseboxes full of household stuff and I was selling it off to keep my head above water. I didn't know how to claim dole or where the office was.

Then one fateful Sunday morning, Martyn had arranged to play tennis with Jimmy, they had been lodgers so why not? I went along too. BIG mistake, Joe went mad and kicked Martyn and I out. That was the nearest I have been to being homeless. Of course Martyn and I didn't really take it seriously enough until 2 in the morning after we had been clubbing, we found ourselves sitting in the car in Newcastle centre and nowhere to go and sleep. We had to go and wake friends up in Gateshead to sleep on their couch and floor. Martyn very quickly bought a house in Jesmond, the posh end of Newcastle, and we lived there for a while. I started to work as a porter at The Avon and Northumbria Hotels on Osborne Road. Life was taking a turn for the better.

I worked with another Porter called Rob who used to keep me howling laughing. He was very straight looking but could be camp and didn't care. He was brilliant at saying just the right thing at the right time. I cracked up every time. For example, the Wallace Arnold coaches used to arrive to stay the night en route to Scotland. It was Rob and I who served the coffee in the lounge after dinner. Loads of old ladies would ask, "Can I take my husband's?" (Coffee.) Rob used to say, "Well, if you don't know by now love."

The two hotels were on opposite sides of the road and a zebra crossing between both receptions. One day we had been sent to tidy up after a party in the Avon Hotel. Rob found a headscarf and popped it into his pocket to hand into Reception later. Our pagers went off just before we got finished so we had to report to the Northumbria Reception over the road. We both exited the Avon Hotel together and just as we were about to cross over the crossing, Rob said "watch this". He held up his hand to stop the traffic and proceeded to do a camp mincing walk across the crossing, but stopped midway to put the headscarf on. I was incapable, hanging off the beacon and crying laughing. The cars were getting annoyed and hooting their horns. I could not have walked if it was to save my life. The best bit was when we arrived at the Northumbria Reception, his face was straight as if nothing had happened. I was the one who got a scathing look for laughing and smirking.

Around this time there was a film crew arrived at the hotels to film 'When the Boat Comes In', with Geordie actor James Bolam. The Conference Room in The Avon Hotel was set up as a dressing room. Rob and I had great fun chatting to the actors and dressers and star spotting around the hotels. We used to snoop through the wardrobe and look at the old costumes. I think Rob enjoyed it far more than me as he was always up in the Hotel Sauna, "entertaining" the actors and dressers. I had to cover for him and would lie very badly that he had been called up to a room to fix something. The dirty little bugga. Ha-ha.

The housekeeper in the hotels was Rena. She didn't have a very good sense of humour, she spits when she talks and she didn't like us at all. Well, one day after getting a mouthful of abuse off her, we decided to teach her a lesson. We caught her and wrapped her up in dirty bed sheets and tied her up with the extension lead off the Hoover's, popped her in a linen basket and wheeled her out into the back street and left her there for an hour. What people must have thought about this moving linen basket in the yard. I still think it's hilarious. We never got any more crap off her after that.

If you think that was cruel, you are so wrong. In the top end of the Northumbria Hotel there was a very nice coffee house. A young lad called Shaun worked in the back kitchen washing up. He was your normal spotty youth, angry red spots, greasy hair, you know the type. One fateful Saturday it was his sixteenth birthday. We got him out in the back street at the back of the coffee house, took a branch off one of the trees and tied his arms along it, a bit like a scarecrow. We frog marched him round to the front of the hotel to where there was a Bus Stop. We waited until the number 33 bus came from town and stopped. Remember this was Jesmond, the posh end of Newcastle, very middle class and twee. We quickly dropped his trousers and boxer shorts and left him standing there whilst the Saturday shoppers got off the bus. It was hilarious! Even Shaun laughed about it later.

Shortly after Martyn and I moved into the Osborne Road, Jesmond flat, Joe came looking for me and as he was in a very bad state, I tried to help him. Martyn wouldn't have anything to do with him. It was from this point that the strain on me was beginning to get me down. Joe used to tell me that he was going to commit suicide, no threats, no going back, he was determined and he knew what method he was going to use but wouldn't tell me how. I tried my utmost to be there for him but over the coming months of taking him to St Nicks Psychiatric Hospital in Gosforth for treatment where I used to be strong right up to the Doctor taking him in for his treatment and then the flood gates opened. I would sob unashamedly in the hallway waiting for him to come out. Well, not long after that, and having moved another twice in a very short time to a multi storey block on the eleventh floor, I lost the plot completely.

I had been drinking Dutch Jenever Gin and I suppose I was quite drunk when I went and stood on the balcony and decided to jump. My family life had folded around my ears, my career had gone up in smoke when I moved to Newcastle, I had no support, and Madge was happily re married and didn't give a shit anyway. Joe was batty as a fruitcake so what was there to live for. I stood and contemplated it, the urge to jump was massive inside my head and it would solve all my problems. There was however a fight going on inside my head, the most of me wanted to jump and end it all but another voice was telling me not to. My head was divided between the devil and the deep blue sea. It was almost as if I was no longer in control. I don't know what drove me to go inside and sit down to try and get my head straight but I did. I rang Joe to tell him what had happened and the next thing the police were at the door.

I went to the Doctors the next day and was seen by a Doctor recommended by Joe who was nutty herself. She explained in layman's terms what had happened. She told me that the borderline between sanity and insanity is a very fine divide and that every stress factor in your life pushes you further towards insanity. I had had too many stress factors and had snapped under the strain. She gave me pills (Valium) that knocked me out for eight days and slowly but surely, I started to claw my way back. Being strongly independent and strong willed, I wasn't prepared to take this lying down so I started to read psychology books in order to understand what was happening. That was it, I moved back to Aycliffe for a while and shared a flat with Carolyn, my sister, before deciding to go abroad.

Desiderata

During my time with Joe, he gave me a framed copy of Desiderata for my birthday. I have included it in this book because at times of great stress it brings you right back down to earth and grounds you. I have found it useful on many occasions.

Go placidly amid the noise and haste, and remember what peace there may be in silence. As far as possible without surrender be on good terms with all persons.

Speak your truth quietly and clearly; and listen to others, even the dull and the ignorant; they too have their story.

Avoid loud and aggressive persons, they are vexations to the spirit.

If you compare yourself with others, you may become vain and bitter;

for always there will be greater and lesser persons than yourself.

Enjoy your achievements as well as your plans.

Keep interested in your own career, however humble; it is a real possession in the changing fortunes of time. Exercise caution in your business affairs; for the world is full of trickery. But let this not blind you to what virtue there is; many persons strive for high ideals; and everywhere life is full of heroism.

Be yourself. Especially, do not feign affection. Neither be cynical about love;

for in the face of all aridity and disenchantment it is as perennial as the grass.

Take kindly the counsel of the years, gracefully surrendering the things of youth.

Nurture strength of spirit to shield you in sudden misfortune. But do not distress yourself with dark imaginings. Many fears are born of fatigue and loneliness.

Beyond a wholesome discipline, be gentle with yourself.

You are a child of the universe, no less than the trees and the star; you have a right to be here. And whether or not it is clear to you, no doubt the universe is unfolding as it should. Therefore, be at peace with God, whatever you conceive Him to be, and whatever your labours and aspirations, in the noisy confusion of life keep peace with your soul.

With all its sham, drudgery, and broken dreams, it is still a beautiful world. Be cheerful. Strive to be happy.

Chapter 6

Freedom Abroad Spain

My first job abroad was working on a Campsite in Costa Brava, Northern Spain, between Lloret de Mar and Tossa de Mar, Camping Cala Llevado, Aire Libre. I was working for Club 18-30 Holidays. I got the job as I spoke School French (very little, even after 6 years at school) and a smattering of self-taught German, so the company sent me to Spain. I loved the job, working outside on the campsite, looking after guests and going on excursions with them, albeit booze fuelled and raucous. My job was as a Security Guard but after seven weeks I became a Rep. It was obvious to me that the other Reps mostly from London and Sheffield who I thought were much more worldly wise than myself, I was the green country boy, were in fact, frightened of the dark, worked themselves up into a frenzy because they thought we could get mixed up with the mafia or put upon by spies. I was totally bemused by all of this and listened intently about these subjects that I had no previous knowledge about. I wasn't troubled in the least. I settled into life as a Rep and I had a brilliant time. I was making money hand over fist, something I had never done before, and as we were taking large groups into bars,

Restaurants and Discos, and we got everything for free. BONUS!!

The excursions were excellent, Disco Tours, Go Cart Racing, and Beach Party, just what I needed to take my mind off events at home. Carefree and sometimes eventful. We had a weekly Beach Party at Santa Christina which was always great fun. Games in the sand, sing-along around the guitar, picnic under the pine trees, it was idyllic. One day after we had eaten our picnic we settled down on the beach for an hour for a snooze in the sun. We were rudely awakened by the most blood curdling scream coming from the rocks. One of the girls had gone to sit on the rocks with her feet in the water but was holding her foot out of the water now with the biggest octopus tightly wrapped around it. I was horrified yet amused by the incident. I laughed until I cried. Someone eventually pulled it off but I would have been useless in the state I was in, weak with laughter.

At the top of the campsite was Bar Victoria, run by Victoria herself and her two sons, Jaime and Jorge. We became great friends and would start and finish our excursions at the bar. Upstairs was a restaurant and downstairs was an open plan cafe with balconies, pool tables and a dance floor. Menu del Dia (meal of the day) was incredibly cheap, on the few occasions we had to pay. There were two lovely Spanish waitresses working in the restaurant, Maria who was a little bugga and came from a small village in Andalucía, and Manoli who was really sweet and polite, the total opposite to Maria. One day Maria came running to look for me to translate at one of her tables. There were a group of welsh boys and they were asking for peaches, I explained to them that the word means penis in Spanish (pecha), hence Maria's distress. So they got their "melocoton" without any more trouble. Maria then hit on the idea that she wanted to know some bad words in English, and you know what my sense of humour is, I taught her to say, "Fuck off, you cunt." I am ashamed as I write this now but not half as ashamed as I was the night it all backfired on me. We had the big bosses across from London to see how we were getting on, so we arranged a big party at Victoria Bar for our guests. It was a brilliant success. At one point I was standing at the bar talking to Paul Staton who was our most senior boss when I felt a tug on my sleeve, it was Maria, "Que dices el?" (What is he saying?)

There was a group of young English lads so I asked what they wanted, they were after sex, so I told Maria that it was very bad what they wanted. She stood there, all 4 foot 6 inches of her, in her waitress outfit complete with tea towel over her arm and screamed at these boys. "Fuck off, you cunt!" I could have crawled under the nearest stone or dropped down a crack in the floor. Paul Staton looked at me bemused and I was just about to recover some composure when Maria, whilst walking up the stairs back to the restaurant, leaned over the balcony and screamed it again.

I never understood the English in Spain. They came for two weeks in the sun but only wanted to go to English bars. I made a beeline for Learning Spanish, making friends with the locals and getting to know how they lived etc. I was speaking Spanish within 2 months and when I wasn't working, I was either down the beach with my Spanish pals or in Lloret partying with them. One day we were down the beach sunbathing and playing with a ball when Eduardo, who taught me Spanish, said he was hungry. I was too so mistakenly thought we were going to get a burger, WRONG!! Off we went into the sea around the rocks and they started to pull whelks and shells off the rocks, and ate them, raw and alive. I nearly puked. By the way, burgers were a new food to me too; being a country boy, we never had access to McDonalds so burgers were a rare treat for tea at home.

Another day, whilst talking about beach stories, I went down the beach alone. At the bottom of Cala Llevado were a number of coves, one of which was a nudist beach. Now remember that my prehistoric parents had bred into us that you had to keep covered up, to the point where I had nightmares about showing my bits. Well, I got installed on this beach, took off my clothes and the liberation was fantastic. I fell asleep for a while in the hot sun and woke up hot and bothered so the dilemma began. Should I or could I walk down the beach naked and have a swim. So I did, it was a bit daunting but I did it. I had a lovely dip and the problem began, I was mortified that the cold water had shrunk Mr Wiggly to baby size. I was absolutely mortified walking back up the beach in the knowledge that if I hid my bits with my hands then it would only draw attention to the problem. Some lessons in life can be so cruel.

There was an incident on the campsite that was worth mentioning and will give you an insight into just what us reps had to put up with. A group of eight youngsters, teenagers, arrived and occupied two tents. They were from North London. On the first night in resort one of the lads rolled down the campsite steps, drunk, and dislocated his shoulder. I had to take him to the doctors and luckily, I got shown how to put it back in if it happened again. I think I put it back in twice before the end of their stay. Now we all know that you would never get an English GP to teach you that would we?

New guests arrived on a Saturday in resort and we went to the Spanish Barbeque on a Monday night. So this group came to the BBQ and we kept an eye on them so that they didn't get too out of order. We got back to the Victoria Bar around eleven and proceeded to party in there. We were back at the campsite so our shift was over, guests were not our responsibility anymore… so we thought! I got woken up at seven am the next morning by one of the workers on the campsite, he had found a body at the bottom of a cliff. I went over and took one look, saw charcoal trousers and white shirt and told the worker that he was a waiter, not one of ours. BUT wait a minute, alarm bells were ringing in my head. I raced down to the tents on my moped and woke up the group of eight. "Are you all here?" I asked.

"No, Johnny never came home last night." I raced back up to the body and by this time an ambulance had been called. I just had time to grab my money bag, knowing that there was no national health and treatment was going to have to be paid for. The ambulance took us straight to Gerona Hospital where I had to prove that I had money to pay before they would touch him. They cleaned him up and packed us back into the ambulance and sent us to Barcelona Hospital. Again, I had to waive the cash. By this time, it wasn't quite ten in the morning and I had already paid out £400 of company money to get this lad seen to. He all the while was still in a coma. I eventually got to a phone and got through to Mickey our Manager and told him what had happened. He assured me that I had done the right thing. This lad eventually came round and was OK, his parents came out to take him home, but get this, and they wouldn't claim the £400 back on Johnny's holiday insurance because it was our fault for getting him drunk!

Another incident, that shook me to the centre of my being, happened in the Victoria Bar one night. We were all having a great night, drinking and dancing, when a girl collapsed and stopped breathing. I only knew basic first aid so started immediately on mouth-to-mouth resuscitation. I was panicking as I was getting no response at all. Eventually she started breathing again, much to my relief, but I was done in, I went out onto the balcony and sobbed my heart out. It had only been a matter of months since I had identified my dead brother and this was all too real for me to manage.

I had a brilliant first season in Costa Brava and was going home with £3000, I was rich. I phoned my friend Harold who had Regan and asked him to get her in and fit and I would have a couple of days hunting on her. I was looking forward to seeing her again. She had been running out on the fell up at Kirby Stephen and prior to me going away, the trotting stallion had knocked the wall down and got in with her and some other mares. We never got her tested but presumed she was in foal. She never produced so she ended up having about a year's holiday. With all the excitement of getting back home and going round to see my friends, it was about ten days before I managed to phone Harold to see how Regan was getting on. He told me that she was dead, hit by lightning. I couldn't believe it. Harold's daughter Jo had brought her down off the fell and had been riding her every day to get her fit. She rode her for 6 days and on the Sunday found her dead in the field. To this day I choke when I drive past that fell, remembering my best horse. You only get one horse in a lifetime like that, and she was mine. At least it would have been quick and she didn't suffer. I am now 63 and if I allow my mind to wander back to this wonderful horse, I still shed a tear for her and will remember her until the day I die, as a great horse, a great friend and a great character.

When I was an old Pro at nude sunbathing, I went on the mainstream nudist beach at Boadella, the other side of Lloret, close to Fanals. We had to go into Lloret to the Club 18-30 office to liquidate our excursion money, so I would disappear afterwards to have a bit of 'ME' time. Most of the time on a beach I will sleep, there is nothing I like better than sleeping under the red-hot sun. It was on one of these occasions that I woke up to see an extremely attractive Dutch lady with her children coming up the beach towards me. They stopped at the towels on the beach closest to me and the lady started to towel dry the children. She bent over in front of me at one point in the proceedings and I was looking straight up her Lady Garden. What happened next turned my stomach. Her hand came down to wipe away a trickle of water from her bum and as she wiped, she left four red "go faster stripes" across it. I nearly puked.

I met a Polish Girl called Wanda (pronounced Vanda not Wander), she was great fun and worked as a Rep for Intasun Holidays. We got on like a house on fire. She was born and bred in Essex and she had exactly the same sense of humour as me. She dyed her hair to the same colour as her uniform, maroon! We had some adventures. One night at Gerona Airport we were wrongly put on Airport Duty together. I had taken some "Slime" with me, fluorescent green sticky stuff. We thought it would be great fun greeting arriving guests with a bit of it hanging out of our noses like a bogey. She had to go one further and borrowed an Airline wheelchair to sit in whilst doing it. It was so funny and a "sackable offence" but we never got found out.

It was around that time that Franco had died in Spain and with the exit of the dictator laws became extremely liberal in Spain. Drugs were legal so we had a little dabble. We managed to get a bit of Charlie from someone in the Victoria Bar and went back to my wooden cabin on the campsite to try it. I hadn't a clue what to do with it but with Wanda we made a couple of lines and snorted it. Now at that time there were a load of Dutch Families in the surrounding chalets and having children they tended to go to bed early. So here was Wanda and I after Victoria Bar, 11–12 midnight, we decided to have sex under the influence of Charlie, the drug that speeds you up. Well, it got rather vigorous and we knew nothing until the bed crashed to the wooden floor with the biggest bang. The Dutch were up, banging on the door, shouting and we lay in a heap laughing. I could hardly show my face the next morning. I only ever took Charlie once more in my life but I can honestly say, "Been there, seen, it, done it, never again!"

One day at Montjuic Park in Barcelona whilst queuing to get on a ride at the funfair, the youth of about 13 years old turned to me with a big spliff in his mouth and said, "Tienes fuego?" (Have you got a light?) I smoked at that time so lit it for him. I thought at the time, this has gone too far. Kids getting high and then riding the funfair. That was the end of my drug era.

Wanda and I decided to get engaged, we announced it at the Orient Express Bar in Lloret courtesy of Jimmy and Eileen the owners. I don't think I was that committed as I never got a ring bought. Here was the girl pressure again, Wanda wanted it, and I wasn't sure. Anyway, here I was cornered, not sure which way to turn so I went to the nearest Gay Bar, El David, in Lloret. I met Jose Munoz from Barcelona. I was smitten but how to tell Wanda? I am not sure how I managed to get it across to her but we all ended up friends and even though Wanda is married, with children, and living on the south coast of UK, we have spoken and will remain lifelong friends.

I moved to Barcelona at the end of the second season in Lloret and moved in with Jose. He was a Pharmacist working in a sweet factory, Mauri, not 200 yards from where we lived on Plaza Joan Cortinas, Bario Bon Pastor, just behind Sagrada Famillia, the unfinished church. I wasn't working so would spend my days exploring The Ramblas and all the tourist spots. I would shop in El Corte de Ingles on Plaza Cataluña. I had a great time. In the evenings, Jose and I would go to the cinema or Theatre with his friends. It was here that I saw the Black Theatre of Prague and Cirque du Soleil, what brilliant shows.

On weekends we would nip down to Sitges on the train for lunch or pop up to Andorra on the coach. I got to see parts of Costa Brava that were off the tourist map. Montserrat and the black Madonna, Gerona, what a magnificent city, all bridges across a river and very baroque, Cadaques and the home of Salvador Dali.

Jose's family were Catalans through and through so it was extremely difficult for me, especially when his eldest sister, Rosi, lived next door to us, but in the next block of flats. Our balconies were adjoined. She would knock on the window to pass in food for us. It was very awkward trying to understand her Spanish accent (broad Catalan). Jose's favourite sister Loli, lived close by and we spend quite a bit of time with her and her husband Angel. They had two daughters Monica and Caroline and a baby son Angelito, who was the demon child from hell. Angelito could get anywhere in the house whilst strapped into his high chair. He would rock it to and fro so that it walked along the marble floor. It had to be seen to be believed. We would use Loli and Angels second home up at Vidreras (Sils) for weekend breaks. They had bought a plot of land and built a swimming pool and a garage. They built as and when they could afford it. Years later on they have now got a very presentable villa with a pool and beautiful gardens.

Whilst working in Costa Brava I obviously got a bit home sick, and psychologically it was having a bit of a toll on me (even though I wasn't consciously aware of it). I started to buy 'The Lads'! Toys which became my family. Mickey and Minnie Mouse lived on my bedside table, they had deck chairs and toys of their own. Mickey had a racing car and a speed boat. Minnie had a dressing table set and a Sony Walkman made out of a matchbox and some wire. If I went away for the day, they expected presents, hence their toys. I loved it and talked about them as if they were human. I would have conversations with friends about Mickey giving me earache about this and that. They thought it was hilarious. By the end of my repping career, I had a whole bunch more of them. Thomas was a Caveman, named after young Thomas from the farm back home. I had been to Barcelona and bought a baby doll that was so lifelike that it had its "bits". Suzy had a lovely knitted shawl and she had a good life until one fateful day I took her down to the beach in Lloret. My mate and I were getting a bit bored with sunbathing, so we went up onto the jetty for a game of pass the ball, only we didn't have a ball, it was pass the Suzy. We threw her higher and higher and caught her from ever increasing distances. We weren't aware that by this time the whole of Lloret beach were sitting up and staring in disbelief, mortified, in our direction. What a hoot. I can just hear Brian Connolly saying in my ear now, "It's a puppet!" I am not sure what happened to Suzy, I lost her along the way somewhere. I have even been back to Barcelona a few times but could not find one like her.

Skiing, Austria

I did two seasons as a Ski Rep in Austria for Club 18-30, they were brilliant. The first season at St Johann in Pongau, and the second season, in Altenmarkt. My first season I arrived on a coach about teatime, and was overawed by the Heidi like beauty of the green slopes, dark wooden chalets, and the magnificent mountains. That was the one and only time I saw it like that because it snowed about ten inches overnight and a whole new beauty took over. This was the first time I had been sent to a resort where I spoke the language, albeit very little, from the onset. I was living in the Sporthaus Pirnbacher which had the resort ski hire downstairs. The first ski lift was thirty yards from the front door. Was I spoilt or what? Only problem was I had to learn to ski before any clients arrived. I had told that London office that I did ski which was only half a lie really. I had been for two lessons on a dry ski slope but I had been ice skating for years so I was sure I could do it. Stuart, another rep working with me, and his Swedish girlfriend, Marrianne, taught me the hard way. They took me up onto the red and black runs and I had to get down. I tell you within a week I was skiing like a professional. I never got to Stuart's standard, he was like a cat on Skis, so fluid and he made it look so easy.

Emi Pirnbacher was the owner of the Pension; she was a force to be reckoned with. FIT wasn't the word for her, she had the body of an Olympic athlete and went cross country skiing every day. I went with her one day and had not a hope of keeping up with her. She was like a steam train on skis. She ran the pension with military precision and took no prisoners. Her husband, Wastel, was a mild-mannered man and Emi would tell all the guests that he was no good in bed. Too old, she would say. She had a secret string of lovers when she went to the Greek Islands in the summer. I don't blame her one jot!

Imagine my utter embarrassment when she walked into the breakfast room one morning, held a bed sheet aloft showing a blood spot, to everyone sat eating breakfast and announced, "Who has been making virgins kaput in my bloody beds?" I could have crawled under the table.

We had a great season with loads of fun. The excursions were fantastic, especially the toboggan run. We would bus it up to the Gasthof on top of the mountain closest to where I lived. We would party in the bar and then come down the toboggan run back to St Johann. Only trouble was that one of us had to go down first as the end of the run came out on a main road. Health and Safety would never have allowed that. The exhilaration coming down that run at speeds of up to sixty miles an hour in the dark was brilliant.

The thermal waters at Bad Hoffgastein were a favourite excursion too. Swimming indoors and outdoors in the thermal waters was just magic for aching muscles. Jumping out of the pool and rolling in the snow, and back into the warm water was great fun. I steered clear of the sauna though, they were mixed, male and female, and naked! I didn't want to risk embarrassing myself.

I used to ski the Three Valleys every Tuesday and take clients. I had a group of Stockton Young Farmers which was close to where I came from, staying in the Pirnbacher. I took them out and they said it was the best ski holiday that they had ever had.

One of my magical moments in Austria was going up in the chair lift one morning, through a forest, after a massive snow fall the previous night, and just gliding through the tranquil silence and the snow laden trees. There are few moments in life when the scenery takes your breath away but this was definitely one. The sun shining, the snow hanging heavy on the branches of the fir trees, and feeling glad to be alive.

At the end of the season, I travelled home in the drivers sleeping compartment on one of the company coaches. I was absolutely shattered, but happy shattered, and slept from Austria all the way to Dover.

Chapter 7

Intasun Winter Work Newcastle

After my first season in Spain, I did half a season working in the Newcastle Reservations office before going off to do my second half of the winter in the Ski Resort. The Intasun office was just outside Jesmond and I took the Club 18-30 calls. The atmosphere in the office was great, there were some real characters working there, some of which had been on my induction course. It was a very relaxed atmosphere and the manager, Pauline, was firm but as long as she got her stats, she was fine. I was naughty, I would phone Jose in Barcelona on the office phone and sit there talking to him in Spanish, Pauline would ask who I was talking to and I would tell her it was another Rep and we were talking Spanish as it was private. She accepted it and I got away with it every time.

There were other Intasun reps working in the office who were home for the winter. Looking back, it was a brilliant place to work as most of the staff were outgoing, positive people. There were a couple of staff who were not quite as outrageous as some of us. One in particular who wore the same purple cardigan every day. I would say, "Christ, she must sleep in the bloody thing!"

Mitch, the Big Manager, I am sure used to despair at the conversations going on in the office between calls. I think secretly he would leave his door open a bit so he could have a laugh. And laugh we did! One girl Debbie, who was a hoot at the best of times, had a call from an Indian man one day. He wanted to take a camp bed with him on the flight and Debbie was trying to explain to him that he could but he would have to check it in with his luggage. He was having none of it, so Debbie was getting frustrated and turned the speakerphone on so we could all hear the conversation. Well, it was absolutely hilarious. How she kept her face and voice straight, I will never know, we were all in fits. The Indian Man was saying, "But, but, but I am wanting to take the bed with me on the flight." I think he thought he could put it up in the aisle and have a sleep on the way there.

We had a flight to Majorca that went out on a Saturday teatime, around 5 pm, from Newcastle Airport, and returned around 10.30 pm. On a couple of occasions, we would quickly see if the flight was full, a couple of hours before it departed, then book any free seats for ourselves and rush up to the Airport and off to Majorca. We would literally fly to Majorca, getting drunk for free en route, as it was Intasun's flight, then charge through customs and duty free in Majorca Airport, get back on the plane and fly home. It was a great buzz going out in town later, tipsy already and when friends asked where we had been to get so tiddly, they didn't believe us when we said "Majorca"!

One such flight, there were about five of us, and as they were free seats, we were scattered all over the plane. One lad Graham came back to where I was sitting and told me that the people who were sitting around him, obviously English, were speaking Spanish. So I went and sat in his seat and listened to the conversations. Well, I don't know who they were meeting in Majorca but they were going to get shagged through the mattress when these girls got there. I went back and told Graham. We howled later when he let on that we knew what they were talking about.

Club 18-30 Office in Soho Square, London

Before going off to my Ski Resort after my first season in Spain I did a little stint in the Club 18-30 office on Soho Square, just off Oxford Street in London. The main office being over in Camden Town. The office was directly opposite the HQ for the Hari Krishnas and they could be seen almost daily chanting and banging their instruments on the street, dressed in their bright orange saris. I was issuing uniform to the Reps so I got to meet quite a number from other resorts. I had installed myself in an old friend's flat, Phil from Newcastle, round at Notting Hill. He didn't mind (I think). He and I would go to parties and out to clubs. I remember standing in one party and thinking to myself, what would Madge make of this? There were gays, prostitutes, Indian people, black people, and lesbians. All new to me, being a country boy but I took it all in my stride.

A Dinner Party we went to was in a flat behind Oxford Street and Phil informed me that it was an American theme, in other words everyone had to make something to contribute to the meal. We chose to do dessert as the only thing that we felt confident to do was cheesecake, made from a packet. Off we went and we had a great night. On the table was the biggest cauldron of chilli con carne, which was new to me. I had never had it before, so I had two large platefuls, delicious! Then they told me it was laced with hashish. No kidding I was tripping for two days afterwards. I didn't remember the rest of the party, I had a hard time concentrating at work the next day, and I didn't give a shite who got what uniform. I certainly learned to look before I leap after that.

I left Club 18-30 after Christmas on my second season in Austria due to lots of reasons but I think I had outgrown the pace of life and the chaotic lifestyle. Jose was with me and we went off to Vienna for a few days. I loved it there, classy and beautiful and oozing culture. We tried to get into the Spanish Riding School but it was fully booked for weeks. So disappointing!

Our accommodation was thrust upon us really. We had arrived at the train station in Vienna from Salzburg. A lady came up to us as we were collecting our cases. "Do you need rooms?" she asked. Well, as a matter of fact we did. She took us to a lovely big town house with enormous rooms. There was a king size Gondola bed and beautiful antique furniture. It was just like being on set for 'The Sound of Music!'. The lady's family had fallen on hard times and she had to let out rooms in her beautiful home to make ends meet. Lucky for us!

There was only one down side of being in Vienna. The fur shops! We hated them! Beautiful, rare animals' skins, sewn together to make coats. Puma, Ocelot, Jaguar. We spat at the windows in disgust.

Intasun Training Programme

During the second half of the winter, having left Club 18-30, I got chance of an interview with Intasun Holidays (International Leisure Group. ILG). They had just recently bought out Club 18-30, so it was like same company, different department. The interview was at their head office in Bromley. I sailed through the interview and got offered a job but I had to attend a training week in Costa Del Sol first.

The training course was in San Pedro at the Hotel Cortijo Blanco. A lovely hotel at the edge of the town, close to the beach, and built as a quadrant, like a castle. With the swimming pool and gardens, in the centre of the quadrant, overlooked by the rooms.

What a week. It was just one great big BONKATHON! Everyone was at it! Far worse than Club 18-30. We worked hard all day learning company practices and procedures, first aid and customer services. But the nights were party, party, party! Sods law found me sharing a room with a lad called Richard. Ex-army, divorced, and thoroughly boring. Conformist, fuddy and well, just boring! Everyone else on the course were characters and party people.

The trainers tried to keep themselves separate from the trainees, but Simon the Head Trainer, made it patently obvious during the training sessions that he fancied me. His eyes would burn into me and it was a bit embarrassing really. Imagine my surprise when he showed up in our bedroom one night towards the start of the training programme. Richard, as straight as a dye, fast asleep in the next bed to mine. I went back with him to his room, diagonally opposite our room, close to Reception. All well and good but trying to get back to our room in the morning, without anyone seeing was damn near impossible, past Reception, past the Dining Room and people having breakfast. Then there was the impossible task of not letting on to Richard, where I had spent the night.

Most nights we all went into Puerto Banus to party. It was brilliant. We went to a party on a yacht, a party in a very posh villa. I loved Joe's Bar at the back of the town which didn't open until 10pm. Brilliant music and atmosphere. The Deejay was like Terence Trent Derby and the music got better and better as the night went on and he smoked more and more whacky baccy (dope).

We met loads of people who were intrigued as to where so many extroverts living it up, were from? This was the life and much better than Club 18-30. The question now was, "Is it just human nature to carry on like sexually liberated dogs on the street or do you really need the banner of Club 18-30?" There were casualties though. One couple, strangers until this training week, got sent home for bonking on a car bonnet outside Reception. Lucky or unlucky for them, it was the trainers that caught them.

There was a very camp lad called Gary on the course. I could not see him as a rep as he looked the type to stand a cry at the faintest distress. He really should have had a skirt on. He was taunting me one day so I grabbed him and threw him in the swimming pool, fully uniformed. Poor lad.

What a fantastic week. I loved it. I thought I had died and gone to heaven.

Chapter 8

Athens

My first season with ILG was working for Lancaster Holidays and I was sent to Athens. I told them I spoke German and Spanish and off I got packed off to Greece. What a culture shock after Spain and it's tourist friendly resorts. Here was a bit of culture, that was strange to me, yet exciting. I spent a few days in Glyphada getting acquainted and then got taken down to resort. I was to spend the summer at Hotel Kalamos Beach, Agios Apostoli, not far from Marathon. The hotel was on a beach overlooking the island of Evia. It was owned and run by Mr Panayiotis Raptis. A lovely fella with a shock of white grey hair. He was very mild mannered but had left his wife for one of his cleaners. Olga, his new spouse was the total opposite of him, loud and aggressive. She had come from a small Greek village and she thought she had reached the pinnacle of her career by being with Mr Raptis. She would bark at the staff and walked round as if she was a queen in a castle. She tried barking at me but to no avail. Once we got it agreed that I was going to be no skivvy I went on to have a brilliant summer. I made some excellent friends and broke my heart at the end of the season when I had to leave.

Agios Apostoli was a village really, a bit of a one-horse town which didn't bother me. Some guests were a bit culture shocked though. It had everything a resort could wish for though, bars, tavernas, gift shops (tatty as they were), an open-air cinema, and a roller-skating rink. The whole place only got busy on a weekend when folk from Athens came for the weekend. The down side of this was that they came with their dogs but invariably could not find the damn thing when it was time to go back to Athens on a Sunday night, so they went without them. We had hordes of feral dogs and it got quite intimidating walking to and from the hotel along the beach road. Mr Raptis had the answer, he would poison meat and leave it out for them. How many times did I wake up to dead dogs all over the hotel lawn. I used to run downstairs in the hotel and tell the manager George, to get shot of them quick before the guests got out of bed.

A very peculiar friendship grew that summer that I wish I could rekindle. When I arrived at Kalamos Beach there were very few people who spoke English as the resort was a weekend retreat for people from Athens, 30 miles away. My saviour was a lovely girl who worked in the bar called Irini, she was Greek but estranged from her Belgian husband and her two sons. She spoke Spanish so I was able to ask her to translate for me and explain things about Greek life that I didn't understand.

At the beginning of the season, all the local boys (kamakis) came into the hotel bar looking for tourist girls to cop off with. One man was an extremely fit looking individual, not unlike Julio Iglesias, but with an arrogance that smacked you in the face at first sight of him. He was called Takis Fafoutis, a star football player, in fact a Captain, with

Kalamos, league division two. Means nothing to me, I hate football.

Let's just say he was about but I never really took much notice of him. That was difficult as he used to swagger into the bar like John Wayne. Then one day whilst I was on duty at the hotel, sitting at my desk with my uniform on, Takis came up to my desk and gave me a rose. That would never ever happen in the north of England where I come from. We became great pals and would knock about together even though I didn't speak Greek and he spoke hardly any English. I was happy to have a mate to go out with and get away from the tourists.

It became a bit of a worry for me because when we were out, if I got a bit bored and decided that I would rather go home, within seconds of me thinking it, Takis would say, "Ella, Pame." (Come on, let's go.) I put it to the test over and over again. He must be telepathic I thought. Now for the spooky bit. Eventually Takis and I could speak enough of each other's language to be able to converse a little. I asked him when his birthday was. 9th June 1955. same as mine. Gemini trait, being able to converse without a language. He was my Gemini twin.

Takis and I were in the Beach Bar and Disco along from the hotel, one night hanging out with friends, as usual. There was a mix of tourist girls and Greek girls but the place wasn't really busy, so it can't have been a weekend. Takis went off to the dance floor and came back with a twinkle in his eye. Some English girl had refused, in a very offensive way, to dance with him and he wanted to know what he could say to her. So I gave him a line! As usual in these situations when I don't put a foot in it, I put two and it comes back to bite me in the arse. The music went quiet momentarily and Takis' voice could be heard by everyone in the Disco shouting "Fuck off, smelly cunt", trying to shout above the din. I was mortified but as usual in these situations I laughed long and loud. That became his signature saying and when we were in English company he would smile and say it, knowing that I would get the blame. Takis taught me all the Greek swear words and later in Crete, my Greek friends were mortified at my dirty vocabulary. It has to be said that foreign swear words are not really sexual, that's only the English that do that. Insults against your mother, parentage and religion are more common in the Med.

I lost touch with him but have heard that he married an English girl called Sandra and moved to England. There was an incident at the end of the season where the staff from the hotel and I met up in Athens. I was standing in Omonia Square with Irini and a few others when Irini asked, "Poo ineh Takis?" (Where is Takis?) Without thinking or looking, I pointed over my shoulder and said, "Here he is," without looking, and there he was coming through the crowds. Spooky eh?

Hotel Kalamos Beach had a little grey-haired receptionist called Maria. She was prim and proper and extremely shockable. I came in from Athens Airport one Monday morning, with all the new guests. to find Maria on the desk. Here's some fun waiting to happen I thought to myself. I stood with Maria and helped her allocate rooms and give out keys. She would ask the guests name and then find them on the list. When Mr and Mrs Mooney gave their name, Maria exclaimed in a loud voice, "I beg your pardon." Mr and Mrs Mooney! Maria was sweating at the gills, I had to lock myself in the back office and actually wet my pants laughing. "Mooney" in Greek is the bad 'C' word for ladies' parts. I can still see this frail little Maria trying to get to grips with what she had heard. Mr and Mrs Mooney were none the wiser as to what they had done wrong.

In Greece they have Name Days and Birthdays. So a friend of Takis, Panayiotis had his name day in his mother's Taverna. I was invited along with Ton Jenner, my Dutch friend who was staying with me at the time. The place was packed out and Ton and I got seated just outside the kitchen door. The village wine was pretty potent and drinking with Ton Jenner who is a world class boozer, I was pissed in no time. The food kept coming and coming. beautiful salads, keftethes, britzoles, papoutzakia, melitzana salata. You name it, we had it. Ton and I were pretty stewed when this apparition appeared from the kitchen. Great big plates with what I thought were crabs on. They weren't, they were sheep heads, split lengthways. The Greeks were spooning out the black brains and the women were fighting over the eyes. I could have puked. What had started out to be a lovely meal was reduced to me nearly throwing up. Yeuk!!!

I had another bad experience in Athens one night. It was a rare night off and I was partying in Athens with Irini and a few others. It got to about 3am in the morning and we decided we were hungry. In Athens you don't go to McDonalds you go down the meat market and eat Patsa. I could throw up typing this. The Meat Market itself stinks of dead animals so you feel less hungry to start with, just entering the venue. My Greek friends ordered the Patsa, entrails soup with great big hunks of bread. When it arrived, I nearly threw up, not only could you see the parts of the entrails in the soup but the stuff stank of shit! The others relished every mouthful. YEUK!!!!!

By far the best part of living so close to Athens was getting to see all the monuments and architecture. I never did get up to the Acropolis but I took folk there every week so I have seen it from every angle. The Flea Market beneath it was my regular Sunday morning excursion, and the nightclubs surrounding were a weekly visit. I got to travel around the islands close to Athens, Evia, Aegina, Poros and Hydra. I was smitten with Greece, fantastic people, warm and friendly, beautiful place, apart from Athens, that is hot, dusty and has a brown cloud over it, pollution. Still nothing in this life is equal to standing in and around Athens and knowing that the ancient civilizations were walking the same streets hundreds of years previously.

Crete

I arrived in Crete in 1985, to work for Intasun, for the start of what was to be three of the happiest years of my life. The first couple of weeks we were in Heraklion which is certainly not the prettiest place to be in, with its hotch-potch of half-finished buildings and the chaos that prevails in every Greek town. We had an induction course out in Linoperamata, east of Heraklion towards Rethymnon and Hania. Then we had to do the excursions that we would be selling to clients. I was absolutely gobsmacked when we got to Knossos, the Minoan temple and ruins. It was here that they kept the Minotaur in the Labyrinth, I remembered it from the cinema in Trimdon all those years ago when I was about eight years old. I felt honoured to be standing there. Crete is steeped in history and the stories fascinated me. We went to the Dikti Caves, up on the Lassithi Plateau, home of Zeus and Rea. I loved the place.

I loved it ten times more when I heard that I was to be head rep in Agios Nikolaos up on the west coast. What a fantastic place, set in the bay of Mirabello, the town is centred around a lake, reputed to be bottomless. I recognised it straight away as the set for the Lotus Eaters which was televised back in the seventies. Just across the mountain there was Elounda where they filmed The Moonspinners with Haley Mills. And just off the coast in Elounda was a fortified island called Spinalonga, which had been a leper colony. I recognised the name immediately as a friend of mine, Alec, had a horse called after it.

Crete has to be one of the most friendly and prettiest islands as Greek Islands go. I love my Cretan friends with a passion and still do. Greek life doesn't come quite as special as Cretan life. As the most southern of the Greek Islands it enjoys better weather, in fact, sunny from March to October in all the three years I was there. It is the largest island and more like a country in itself. Zorba the Greek was filmed in the harbour at Hania, close to the Samaria Gorge. The Bounty advert "A taste of paradise" was made in Vai.

It didn't take long to suss the place out. I have an aversion to English bars and in any resort, I prefer to do as the locals do. I found that in Ag. Nik. most of the English bars were serving "bomba" drinks (industrial alcohol). Cheap alternatives to named brands. As I had ulcers I used to be crippled for days if I drank them. So my favourite places were seldom the favourites of the other reps.

I had a shared flat, with a rep called Julia, at the back of the town overlooking a natural gulley. It was close enough to town but far enough away to give us peace and quiet after a night at the airport. How wrong we were. George the owner didn't tell us that there was to be building work going on at the next block of flats down from us. Nor did he warn us that the workmen would wait especially until we had been at the airport all night and were trying to catch up on sleep before they started blasting out the foundations with dynamite. Our windows rattled, we thought they were coming through. It was like living on a bomb site. We had the nightmare for weeks. It was an impossible situation to be in, but God smiled on me and I got out of the situation.

I was riding down the Disco Street behind the main shopping street one afternoon when I spotted the most handsome Greek man. He almost spotted me at exactly the same time, our eyes met. I stopped and said hello and a few words, he had to get back to work and so did I, so we arranged to meet for coffee later. His name was Manolis (like the rest of Cretan men, most islands have their own names like its Spiros in Corfu, etc.). In those days he looked like a young Andrea Boccelli. He had a shop on the main street selling arty jewellery and ceramics. His parents Maria and Petros lived above the shop with his sister, Zambia. She was as ginger as he was black haired. Petros was a dead ringer for Charlie Chaplin, small framed and a black moustache. Petros' sister, Evangalia, a grey-haired old lady dressed in black, stayed with them most of the time, even though she had her own place up in the mountains at a place called Kritsa. Evangalia, or Thia (aunty), had never been married and was never married due to having a hysterectomy operation when she was 24. She was extremely stern looking but I had some fun teasing her. I would pull up outside the shop, very quietly, on my moped and pinch her bottom as she stood with her back to the road. She would berate me with her mock stern demeanour but secretly I could see through her and she would be loving every minute of it. She had never learned to read or write and had devoted her life to her brother's family, Manolis and Zambia. I would ask her to come out dancing in the bars with us and she would either go along with me or tell me to "asto dialo" (Go to hell). I bought her a watch from duty free and she kept it in her purse. She couldn't even tell the time. I had such a problem with her trying to show her how to use Euros in later life, she had spent a lifetime with Drachmas.

I moved in with Manolis, he had a very old and interesting house up the hill from the OTE Telephone Office, not far from the shop. It was the done thing in Crete that sons left the family home at 18 years of age. The house was on a steep hill and you had to go up some steps onto the stoop, open the side window by the door and put your hand inside to open the door. We never ever locked it. Inside the door you walked along a hallway about eight yards long, then up half a dozen more steps which went round a corner and brought you onto the only level of this house. To the right was a dining room with French windows onto a small balcony overlooking the steep front street, to the left the sitting room and straight on to the only bedroom (single). You had to go through the French windows in the lounge to outside and across the patio to the kitchen, or diagonally across to the right to the toilet and bathroom. The bath had a shower attachment but it was a sit up and beg affair.

The furniture was extremely old but comfortable and we mucked along beautifully in this quaint little Spiti (house). Manolis was in the amateur dramatics and on the town council, as well as an excellent artist. He could paint and draw beautiful pictures. If I had to describe Manolis now I would say that he is dark and handsome, similar to Andrea Boccelli, but his redeeming feature is that he is a thoroughly beautiful person, inside and out. Open hearted, open minded and a brilliant sense of humour. I will love him until the day I die but I couldn't go back and live with him. I have my reasons. I spent three extremely happy years with him in Crete and in the winter, we would go to Athens, Berlin, England for one winter and he came with me to Benidorm too.

Just outside Agios Nikolaos, heading east, there is a fantastic bay and a village called Kalo Horio (beautiful village). I much preferred the lovely sweeping cove there with the brilliant Taverna across the road run by Dimitri and Voula and Janni and his wife. The food was just "to die for"! The beach had a ski school run by Manolis (yet another), who was Burt Reynolds' stunt double. He drove a black beach buggy, spoke perfect English, and was great fun. I would go along on my moped or catch a bus along. I even took 'The Lads' along in the wire basket of my moped. Mickey and Minnie were by this time squatting in Madge's loft so I had a whole new set. Fanos was a clown made from jute sackcloth with coloured patches sewn on. He had been a present from Manolis' shop and I still have him to this day. Brian was a magnificent Parrot made of yellow and blue felt, and sitting on a perch with a spring. Brian would hang from the ski school hut and look very at home in the wind. I had bar towels that I would place the others on and give them a bottle of beer each. Folk on the beach loved it, so did I!

Around about the third year in Crete I got myself a 350cc Honda motorbike with drop handlebars. It was brilliant driving it around in flip flops and a pair of shorts. There was no requirement to wear a helmet. I discovered new treasures in Crete which were out of my reach on a moped. I blasted down the national road at 80 mph one day which was exhilarating but painful when a wasp hit my bare nipple, OUCH! I found a track which led across the hills to the left of the road just before the town of Neapolis, I used it as my scrambling track. It was brilliant. I went up to Kritsa one day which is in the mountains overlooking Ag. Nik. I found my way to the ancient ruins of Lato which were fascinating. I stood in the ruins surveying the surrounding countryside and all of a sudden realised that someone had done exactly the same thing all those hundreds of years ago. It was an eerie feeling but one I will never forget.

I continued uphill from the back of Kritsa and found myself on a plateau, far more primitive than the Lassithi Plateau, and its windmills, which must have been just west of where I was. It looked for all the world like a scene from a western. A lonely ancient Taverna with decrepit old chairs outside. Tumble weeds blowing about. It was amazing.

Petros died after my first season in Crete. He had taken ill and ended up in hospital in Athens as the hospital in Ag. Nik. was ill equipped to deal with him. I had gone out to Agadir in Morocco for seven weeks to look after the resort before the summer staff arrived. I was shocked when Manolis phoned me to tell me and I was disappointed that I could not be there for him in his hour of need. I managed to get back to Crete for the memorial service a month later. It was very, very sad. Maria went into decline and from that time onwards, all she wanted was to go and join Petros. She lived quite a few years later but she went from being a large robust woman to a little frail old lady extremely quickly. Thia (Evangalia), on the other hand, worked her fingers to the bone trying to keep the family together. Manolis seemed to be coping with the death of his father but told me the story of how he had gone to Athens to bring the coffin and body back. God, they were primitive, or were they just realistic. In the UK it would be all done underhand so that the family didn't have to deal with it. I won't go into details but it hadn't been an experience to relish.

We had a very cushy number as far as clients were concerned in Crete. Most people were self-sufficient and either came for the sun or to discover the history and architecture and archaeological sites. We had very few run ins with the police or the hospital. So each of the three seasons I was there was pretty much the same as the one before.

I did spend a few weeks teaching English in a lovely school in Neapolis. Rena Markakis, who owned the school, was a friend of Manolis. It was an absolute delight to teach these lovely Greek kids who wanted to learn. They were obedient and worked hard to achieve the tasks I set them. I must have been smitten because my past record of getting foreigners to swear went right out of the window. They had their books, which I had to adhere to, and take them through each exercise, but the best bit was when we had completed them, the kids would practice speaking English to me. It was brilliant.

I went to Santorini a couple of times whilst living in Crete. The volcanic island was a short ferry trip away. It was nowhere near like Crete and had its own unique architecture. The town of Santorini is reached by cable car, or steep steps running up the side of the mountain from the sea. The views are spectacular. From the town you can see where the crater of the volcano was as the little islands form a massive circle in the sea. It must have been one hell of a blast when it went off. It is reputed that the eruption sent a tidal wave across to Crete and this is what wiped out the Minoan civilization.

Thia Evangalia at 94 was bed ridden and became like a stunt double for E.T., the extra-terrestrial in later years, with her big bum and work worn face. She never lost her sense of humour and I always threatened to take her dancing down the disco. I told her that only the good die young so she must have been a bad bugga in her time to have lasted this long. She died in 2009, a little old lady. Manolis looked after her until the end. She is a great loss to the Sgouros family. This woman who used to walk all the way up to Kritsa, all six miles uphill, carrying Manolis as a child.

I told Manolis in July 1987 that this would be my last season working in Crete. I left at the end of October. I was OK about leaving as I had already got used to the decision. Manolis hadn't come to terms with it so I felt extremely guilty about the hurt on his face as I waited with my suitcases to go to the airport.

Gibraltar

I went to work in Gibraltar two winters but only did half a season each time. Intasun only had the two hotels, Calleta Palace and Gibraltar Beach. The first year I lived in the Calleta Palace Hotel behind the rock. It was extremely old fashioned, about fifty years out of date, as was Gib itself. A little bit of England in the sun! That's not what I would call it. I used to say, Gibraltarians, living proof that the Spanish fuck monkeys! They were hard work, small minded and extremely patriotic. They thought that they were more British than we were. I thought, yes, you are really, sitting there talking Spanish all day.

I had a lovely girl from Glasgow working with me, Sonia. She was half Italian and her family had restaurants. She really was great fun and we kept each other sane.

We had fun at the airport each transfer day with planes trying to land in the wind on the tiny little landing strip that terminated in the sea. It was nothing for planes to take two or three attempts at landing, the cross winds would have the planes swinging in the wind like yoyos.

Our agents were Exchange Travel on the main street, run by Ken Jones. I used to answer the phone, "Sex change travel, how can I help you." I said it quick so that the caller didn't really get time to pick up on it but we had a great laugh in the office. There were a couple of Gib girls in the office but we worked mainly with Nuria, a small dark girl, who was great fun. I came into the front office quietly one day and there was Nuria leaning over the desk, so I smacked her arse quite hard, for a laugh. Imagine my face when she turned round and it wasn't Nuria. It was another girl, also called Nuria from another office and she was livid. I apologised profusely and tried to explain what had happened. She would not hear any of it. Her pet lip was out and it was staying out. I walked away from her mid-sentence in the end, sad bitch. Ken apologised to me later and told me that she was always like that. No sense of fun. I decided that she deserved a good wallop after all.

Sonia and I were coming round the rock in a taxi one day on the way back from the office. We had heard that there was a British ship in port and that the sailors were on shore leave.

We were getting back to the hotel to avoid the crowds in town (it's only a small place). En route to the hotel we passed a couple of young women we thought, skirts up to their panty line and necklines down to their navels. Looking to all the world like Working Girls. I passed a comment to Sonia along the lines of, "You can tell there is a ship in, the girls are out in force." We had a little chuckle about it. When we got back to the Calleta Palace I walked inside and could not understand where Sonia had got to. She eventually came in from outside with a very red face. The taxi driver had stopped her and given her a mouthful for my comment, saying that one of the girls was his fourteen-year-old niece. I ran outside to try and catch him but he had gone. I wanted to tell him that he should go and get his niece and get some clothes on her if that is how she goes around with a ship full of sailors in dock. What a spineless bastard, telling poor Sonia instead of me.

There was a ten-seater plane that was used to take tourists across to Tangiers. I went a couple of times, it was like sitting in a wobbly old deck chair and getting buffeted about. I wasn't very enamoured with Tangiers, it was hot, busy, and noisy and not at all like Agadir.

My top favourite excursion was the Dolphin Safari. A fella called Mike would take us out into the straits on his catamaran and we would see scores of dolphins that came right up to us. They would race the boat and take fish from our hands. They really were special. We never got to see any whales but were told that they could be spotted quite often in the straits.

A very peculiar thing happened to me one day in Gib. I was travelling around the rock in a bus full of tourists taking them to the airport. I was staring across the straits to the Atlas

Mountains of Morocco, thinking of nothing in particular when bang, a thought came into my head, "You have won the Premium Bonds!" It wasn't a hopeful thought, it was a definite assurance that I had won. I rang Madge at the end of the transfer and asked if there was any post for me. There's one from St Anne's, she said. That was it, I had won £500. How spooky is that?

One of the best days of my life was an excursion up to Jerez and The Spanish Riding School. The journey itself was pure joy as it took us across the southern Spain savannas with huge herds of cattle being plagued with Egrets. This is where the fighting bulls were bred for the bullring. It was novel to see them in the pastures with egrets walking up and down their backs picking ticks out of their coats. Jerez itself is a very clean and unique town. Beautiful little casas (houses) with quaint gardens. This is where the sherry is made so there are a number of Bodegas. We had a guided tour of one and I was very appreciative that they stuck to the traditional methods, huge wooden barrels piled up on top of each other.

The Spanish Riding School surpassed all previous knowledge and expectations. We had lunch served to us in the auditorium and watched as these beautiful Andalician stallions performed dressage to classical music. I cried because it was so beautiful. Certainly, a once-in-a-lifetime experience!

Benidorm, Spain

After my second summer in Crete, I went to do half a winter season in Benidorm. It was a big mistake to go back to the mass tourism of Spain after the quaint charm of Greece.

The hundreds of massive skyscraper hotels with hundreds of rooms, all set out along straight roads were a far cry from rural roads and small hotels of Crete. I hated it with a vengeance.

There is no Spanish culture in Benidorm. You have to travel miles outside to get Tapas or a decent Spanish meal. The burger bars, English Bars, Dutch Bars, German Bars. A taste of your own country in the sun. AWFUL!!!

The rep's accommodation was even more awful. Dirty, damp, and overcrowded. Manolis was with me so we had to sleep in a single bed together. A week after I arrived in resort a friend Sue from Crete arrived to work with me. As she was coming up the stairs to the flat, I was shouting down, get out whilst you can. It's awful. We laughed at the time but looking back, I don't know why we stayed.

The Reps were a mixed bag too. Dragan was a Yugoslavian lad, very tall and slim with a definite air of Vincent Price the actor about him. He and I had to share a moped to get to work. His dirty habit of soaking in the bath whilst smoking and flicking the ash over the side onto the floor was intolerable. Mind you, not half as bad as Evie, a Scottish girl. She used to leave her used sanitary towel, sunny side up on the side of the bath. Sue forbade me to say anything. Being an ex-farmer, I can cope with most things, but that really did turn my stomach.

I am not going to regale you with any stories from Benidorm, even though I made a TV programme there for World in Action, about the old age pensioners who came there to stay the whole winter, to avoid the cold in the UK.

Chapter 9

Rhodes

Summer 1988 I had taken promotion with Intasun to Resort Controller, working in Rhodes with Area Manager, Sue. We had twenty-two reps and about five Kiddie Reps to manage between us. I loved the challenge, the new resort to discover and the buzz of the new responsibilities. I had to plan the training programme and train the new reps. It was a brilliant challenge after my duties in Crete.

My brother Alan had worked in Rhodes and had explained the layout of the island and Rhodes town. I found Rhodes to be quite unlike anywhere else I had been in Greece. Quite cosmopolitan, less friendly than Crete, but altogether more up to date with larger hotels and more adapted for tourism. Most of the Rhodians were in fact Athenians and only came over to make money in the summer.

I found a large apartment along Soufouli Street at the back of Rhodes Town close to Monte Smith. It was behind a supermarket so not far to go for groceries. An old friend, Marion Bacon (ex-BBC), moved in with me as it would help with the rent. She was working as Office Manager but didn't stay long as it didn't suit her, so another friend of mine Nicky came and took over the job and the spare room in my flat.

'Nicky No Eyes' had worked with me in Athens so we knew each other well. She would laugh and her eyes would completely disappear, hence the nickname.

Our agents were Traveland and were much more organised than our agents in Crete. Sue and I shared an office on the second floor, within Traveland, to run the Intasun part of ILG and upstairs there was Carmel who ran Lancaster and Global. Club 18-30 were right up on the top floor. The reps had their own room in the basement so it was a brilliant and far more efficient setup than Crete, except that Sue and Carmel didn't get on. It's a woman thing, I had learned years before that two horses don't agree in the same stable and likewise two women don't agree in the same kitchen.

I had a company car, a little old Fiat with a brilliant sound system in it. I soon took to disappearing off down to Lindos, the traffic free village on the west coast. It was a haven after the hustle and bustle of Rhodes town. We had properties in Lindos and reps so I had an excuse to be there. We also had a campsite over in Lardos which wasn't far. I had to keep a bit of distance from my reps so I made friends with an excellent girl called Laura from Global Holidays. Laura was the plainest of girls to look at, short brown hair cut in a bob. Quite tubby and talked with an innocent quiet voice. Quiet she was NOT!! On my first night out with her we were walking up to Lindos by Night Bar when Laura dragged us up a back alley and showed us her Tina Turner impression. She rolled her skirt up at the waistband and strutted round the street singing, "Simply the best." I was crying with laughter. It was brilliant!

All the ILG reps in Lindos shared an old ramshackle house towards the back of the village. Close to the car park where arriving guests were dropped off with their luggage.

Guests were walked through to their accommodation and their luggage was delivered with a motorised Tuk Tuk. Imagine their surprise when they were asked to wait a minute outside the rep's house whist the reps on duty showed two people to their villa. The remaining guests heard the energetic noisy lovemaking from the room behind them and the voice exclaiming, "I know you are coming, you know you are coming, we don't want the whole fucking village to know you are coming." It was Laura!·

One of my other allies was a rep called Maz, she was the choreographer for our rep's gang show (Cabaret). Maz and I got on like a house on fire right from the word go. Sue the Area Manager hated this as Maz was five foot two with blonde hair and blue eyes, a perfect figure, whilst Sue was frumpy to the extreme. Maz used to be a Young & Lively Rep so knew every trick in the book, and we had both been Club 18-30 Reps so we were kindred spirits. Sue had a vendetta against Maz right from the word go. I thought it was comical. Why women do this I don't know, put so much energy into something they have little or no control over. Anyway, I let them get on with it. Maz produced an excellent Reps Cabaret, very funny, very professional and certainly an asset to the team of reps we had.

Maz and I would have adventures together unbeknown to Sue. We would go down the beach, out drinking, in fact we became firm friends and remain as such to this day. Unbeknown to me we both had similar backgrounds and came from families of five. Maz had a very dashing boyfriend when I first met her. Janni was about six foot six and a captain in the Greek Army. We all went for a Chinese meal in Ixia, one night, and Maz and I wanted duck, but every time we said the word duck, we ducked our heads as if something had been thrown at us. It was hilarious and made even more hilarious as Janni hadn't a clue what the joke was. We cried with laughter.

Another funny night with Maz was when we went into a bar close to the office. It was early doors and we were the only two at the bar. The owner of the bar gave me a trick pack of cards and when I opened the pack, I got an electric shock. I hate electric so wasn't very pleased. I was still getting over the shock when the owners dog jumped up at my leg. I shot out of my chair and banged my head on the overhead glass rack. Maz was in stitches, as was I when I eventually took stock of the situation.

Later that night we ended up in a small bar, called Valentinos, in the old part of Rhodes town. We loved it as there was a very camp barman who would dance on the bar and swing the hanging lights around his head as if they were earrings. We had already had quite a number of drinks and here we were sitting at the bar having brandies. Just opposite us was a man sitting in the corner, not six foot from where we were sitting. He looked German so in our drunken state we presumed he was German. Maz turned to me and said, "Isn't he ugly?" I agreed and added that he looked like one of those Cabbage Patch Dolls with the squidgy faces. He could hear this conversation whilst we were having it. Maz decided to tell him that he was ugly and laid into him, assuming all the while that he didn't understand. Well, we nearly fell off our stools when five minutes later he ordered another drink from the barman, in perfect ENGLISH! We still tell the story today.

There were two incidents of note that I should tell you about, but firstly, I spent most of my time in Rhodes getting

English tourists out of jail, hospital, police custody, etc. It was a joke, I knew all the policemen and court officials by name. My opinion on the matter was that we had sold these idiots a holiday and we weren't a nursemaid service. Hospitals were acceptable but Police and Jail were extremely time consuming, totally unnecessary, and stopped me doing my job.

One day in my office, a rep Julie from Faliraki rang me to say that she had a man travelling alone in the Illiada Apartments. He was a bit strange, and running naked around the apartment block, and she thought it best that he get transferred to an apartment in town, where he could be kept an eye on. Illiada Apartments were set in an olive grove outside of Faliraki, and Julie being an ex-nurse, I trusted her judgment. So I made the arrangements for him to go to The Magic Isle Apartments in Rhodes Town, which just happened to be owned by our company Doctor. The man got a taxi and I thought that was the end of it.

Later that afternoon I got a phone call from the Magic Isle to say that someone has been flashing in the apartments. The penny didn't drop immediately, I went racing over there to sort it out. Reception in the Magic Isle was in uproar. I can't tell you how many guests wanted transferring to another apartment. I made a few enquiries at Reception and with guests in the bar area to see what had happened. I eventually went over to a group of lads who were sitting with the culprit. I assumed that they were all travelling together, but no, this was the man from Faliraki! The other lads were just keeping him there until I arrived. I had a stern word with this man and told him that if he needed a prostitute there was the Tulip Bar in town or hundreds of bars where he could cop off. I explained that if he was to get evicted from this apartment, Intasun were under no obligation to re house him. He said he understood and apologised.

I then went to the other guests and told them that it wouldn't happen again and got them settled down. I was just having a word at Reception when this man came and asked if he could have a word. I took him outside and he proceeded to tell me how they were making a film about him called Daft Arthur scores, and the producer was using his own daughter. I was totally bemused, you know what my sense of humour is like. I asked him who Arthur was and her told me it was him. So I told him again to behave himself and went back to the office. I had to report major incidents like this to our London office and I sat on the telex rattling off the story whilst telling Sue. We were howling laughing but the smile was soon wiped off our faces when the phone rang and Magic Isle reported that he had flashed again in the restaurant across the road from them. I rang John Sotiris, the company doctor, and explained the situation. He said to get him to the hospital and he would meet me there. Then at the last minute he changed that to phone me from the hospital once you are there with him, and he would come up. I went across to Magic Isle with strict instructions to NOT put him in my car but to get a taxi. I made my way to the restaurant and there was Daft Arthur sat on a table behind two girls, who happened to be German. The waiters were gesticulating wildly behind Arthur for me to get him out of there. I sat down and asked what had been going on? He said that he had heard the German girls talking about him so I asked the multi-million-dollar question. "Do you speak German Arthur?"

"NO," he replied. I then told him that I needed him to come with me to the hospital, but I would give him a lift providing he sits in the back seat and behaves himself. He agreed to do that. On the way to the hospital, he told me about his taxi journey from Faliraki that morning, how the crowds were lining the streets and cheering as he passed. At one point some children running around in the street were yelling and he said, "There they are again." I couldn't get to the hospital quick enough. On arrival I couldn't see John Sotiris anywhere so I panicked a bit, then realised that he had told me to ring him once I was there. I sat Arthur on a bench next to some patients who were smoking. If you have never been to a Greek Hospital, the patients walk around freely with their saline drip held up high and a cigarette. There were about four such patients on this bench and they were all making circular movements around their heads to indicate that they thought this man was mental. I told them to watch him and ran to the kiosk and phoned Doctor John. Well, Dr John spoke to this man for less than five minutes and put him in a straitjacket. Relief! Oh no! It turned out that this man was an alcoholic and had been on a drying out programme in Glasgow. He had come on holiday and got his pills all out of sync and started drinking again. So his mind was taking peculiar paths. And to top it all, he was travelling without any insurance so no means to pay for the hospital treatment nor an air ambulance to get him home. We rang his mother who sighed and said, "Oh no, not again," and refused to have anything to do with him. So we eventually got an insurance company to take up the case and got him home.

The next incident. We got a phone call in the office one Thursday, from the Airport, to say that one of our passengers from the Tuesday flight had been left at the airport. Our flights went out on a Tuesday and a Friday so no big deal to put them on a flight on Friday, but we were intrigued to know how someone could be in the airport for more than 24 hours undetected. I went down to the airport to find that this man had been asleep in the toilets and missed his flight. He was an insipid character and I took an instant dislike to him. I took him to the Solemar Hotel in Ixia and told him that we would put him on a flight the next day, Friday. Well, he never made the flight on Friday as he was too pissed on his bed to get up and go to the airport. We knew that he would not be allowed to fly in that state. It turned out that he was an ex "Dilly Boy", a male prostitute from Piccadilly in London, and an alcoholic to boot. Yet again, travelling alone without insurance. The following Tuesday he was far too bladdered to fly. I went to the Hotel and saw him lying in a stupor on his bed and I just wanted to punch the idiot. We eventually got him away on the Friday flight with an escort, but all this stress was totally unavoidable.

One week in Rhodes we had two men keel over with heart attacks in the shower. As it was peak season, we joked that it was one way of getting over our overbooking problem. The second one was a farce. The man had been travelling with his girlfriend, not his wife. The girlfriend scarpered as soon as he died. As with all these cases we report them to London office and arrangements are made with the insurance company, as with the first case. In this case the man's daughter wanted to come out and escort the coffin back. Well, in Greece, due to the heat, bodies are buried within 24 hours of them dying so there is no such thing as a chapel of rest. So this man's body was put in a coffin and held at the coffin makers yard just outside Ixia. The daughter went ballistic! I tried to explain but she was having none of it. In my mind she was the one who should have looked into the matter in the first place and this was all her fault. If she had kept her bloody nose out of it, the body could have gone home days ago and end of story. But you can't tell them that. Unfortunately, the day the bodies were to go home, I also had a man in prison due out on the same flight, who just happened to make it by the skin of his teeth, and my mother and aunty on the same flight. Look at this from my point of view readers, I wanted to see my mother and aunty off but had to race up to Rhodes Town Prison to get an idiot out who had thrown a scaffolding bar down the steps of a disco in Faliraki and injured eight people, he stood in court saying, "It wasn't me, it wasn't me," even though there were a number of witnesses who saw him do it. I had to get two stiffs in the hold of the plane but one had arrived without any paperwork, yes, the one whose daughter was travelling with him. It was utter chaos. I stood after the flight went out and thought, "Why the hell do I do this job?"

It was one night in Lindos by Night with Laura that I met Kevin. he was on holiday with his mother after splitting up with his other half. I wasn't really looking to meet anyone having just left Manolis, and having been seeing Mikalis from the Sun Bar in Lindos, and to tell the truth he didn't appear at first sight to be that faceable. He was in the bar with a couple of other lads and they all came down to Acropolis Disco with us. At one point in the evening, I was sitting on a step in the disco when Kevin came and sat beside me. He asked if I was gay and I told him yes. He was too so we ended up spending the rest of his holiday together. We got along brilliantly and I met his mother, Pat. I even moved them into my flat and took them to the airport on the night of their departure. To cut a long story short, Kevin went home, put his house up for sale, that he had shared with Jimmy his ex, with his father as power of attorney, then came back to Rhodes to spend the summer with me. I found him a job with another Tour Operator and we proceeded to spend an idyllic summer together. I was smitten. He was good looking, easy going, and a great friend to be with. There was no pressure from either side. I loved being with him but equally never cramped his style. If we went out on a night and I was tired, I would come home and leave him out partying. I trusted him implicitly… until an old friend Phil came out on holiday. I was working hard so Kevin and Phil would go to the beach together and one day the inevitable happened. At least Kevin had the balls to tell me. I forgave him but it did rankle. I never spoke to Phil again. What bad manners, he was a guest in my house, so he overstepped the mark, well and truly!

We proceeded to have an excellent summer together. His family came out and stayed, his mother and father two or three times. We synchronised our days off and spent long lazy days on the beaches all over the island. Some good friends of mine from Newcastle had gone to Turkey for a holiday and got bored so they chartered a yacht and came over to Rhodes for a few days to see me. They got on well with Kevin. Pat and Terry, Kevin's parents went to neighbouring island of Kos and we went over and spent the day with them. It really was a long hot idyllic summer. Hard work but playing just as hard too, and I couldn't have been more happy. New job, new life, new love!

Kevin's callous departure from my life had a massive impact on my sanity. It was the second year in Rhodes, after our trip to India and a stint in Gibraltar. I never understood it until after therapy. Christmas in most people's minds is a time for family and loved ones BUT my concept of it was hardship and heartache after what had happened with my father (remember I couldn't even talk about it then). Kevin arrived in Gibraltar with flyers from an Estate Agent in Chester, wanting me to buy a property with him. Remember that he had run out on Jimmy just eight months prior.

My whole being wanted to conform but my inner voice told me I was stupid if I did. Anyway, I wasn't ready to come back to the UK and face my demons, and felt like I was getting railroaded into it. I was backed up into a corner and couldn't see the escape. Kevin took his own slant on the situation and went home to the UK. I had not a hope in hell of being able to explain the situation to him so I had just to accept the situation. I was absolutely and utterly disappointed, and that statement describes how I feel today about my parents. My parents had pushed me into a dark place and now here was Kevin pushing me into another one. What had I done to deserve it? I must have done something because it kept happening to me. I lost the plot and had to get away from Gibraltar. I needed time to get my head around what had happened, even though I had no chance of doing so as the past was still locked tight inside me and I hadn't the guts to deal with it. The most I could hope for was that when I got back to Rhodes in March, Kevin and I could pick up where we had left off.

My second year in Rhodes was a complete disaster after that. I lost the will to live, I hated my job, and I couldn't wait to get away from it. Intasun sent me to Israel for six weeks at the start of the season to get the resort up and running for the reps. That was a real bind as my whole heart wanted to be back in Rhodes where Kevin was and get back on an even keel with him. I eventually got to Rhodes and Kevin was there working at the airport on my arrival. I went over and spoke to him. He was obviously embarrassed by my presence as he made some inane remark about having lost some clients. I could see that any kind of relationship was going to be difficult for me. In my mind, I had taken him in, found him a job and shared my concessionary holiday to India with him, so he was going to have to make more effort than I was. I got buried in the job as the six weeks in Israel meant that I had a lot of catching up to do. I tried on numerous occasions to get friendly with Kevin again, we even went to the beach together a few times. The strain was exploding my head. Well, after a few scuffles with him I made supper for him one night and he told me that he had to do a shift at the airport for someone. He left my house early to go. It wasn't until the next day, I was driving through Faliraki and saw his car parked outside an apartment block. I stopped and rang his office to report it, thinking that it could have been stolen. His office told me that he had gone home to the UK the night before. I was heartbroken. It came up in Therapy that he had done exactly what my spineless father had done. Left without a word! Of course I turned this in on myself, another load of baggage to carry around with the shit that was already locked away in my head. And just for your info, dear readers, I have been on my own ever since. It's now 2012 and that makes it 24 years.

Chapter 10

Israel

I went to Israel three times in all. The first time was a hoot. I got called from our London office asking me to go and set up the resort prior to the summer reps arriving. It was at the time of Salaman Rushdie's controversial book, The Satanic Verses. I was told not to mention it. I flew British Airways, Heathrow to Tel Aviv. I was really quite ignorant about Jewish faith and culture but I did know that they don't eat pork. Good old BA, what was the in-flight meal, Roast Pork! That was the funny bit. The very un-funny bit was that the moment the plane levels out after take-off, all the Jews are up at the back of the plane praying and bowing. I panicked, I thought the distribution of weight in the aircraft would cause a crash. I was only too pleased to arrive in Tel Aviv.

I was met and taken to the Blue Bay Hotel in Natanya, where I lived for the duration of my stay. Natanya was a concrete jungle but the Hotel was just north and had marvellous sea views. From the start I was aware of the imbalance of human rights. There were Arab men working as chamber maids in the hotel. I made friends with a couple of waiters, Samir and Adnan, and they started to give me an overall impression of life in Israel from the Arab perspective.

I meanwhile was taking it in from the Jewish side as I was working with them. The Agents office (Ofakim) was in Tel Aviv, and they were extremely helpful. I found it a bit daunting trying to work with shoot outs and bombings going on all around me. I never really encountered any first hand but we were always aware that something was going on all around us. We did have a couple of incidents where tour busses got stoned and our guests hurt. These incidents were always dealt with quickly and the Ministry for Tourism were extremely keen to keep the incidents quiet. I had to go to Jerusalem twice a week and this was the hub of most of the trouble.

The job was easy enough as a lot of people arriving were Jewish or religious. The holy land tour was what most people came for. One Jewish man even came out on holiday to die there. That was a bit daunting for me, it meant that I couldn't sell him any excursions. I found it a bit of a fairy story, I must admit. I have never been religious. I went to the Gardens of Gethsemane, The Sea of Galilee, Nazareth the birthplace of Jesus, The Dead Sea. I enjoyed seeing it all but found it a bit of a mixture of emotions with so much religious aggression going on around me. A bit of a joke really, if this is what religion does for the world, then I want nothing to do with it.

My second trip to Israel, I was determined to see the other side of the coin. I asked Adnan, a waiter from the Blue Bay, if I could come to his house and see how they lived. He lived out at Tulkarm and being Arab, he lived with his extended family. His father had four wives and between them Adnan had loads of brothers and sisters. Now in Israel there is a colour coding of number plates on cars, blue plates for Arabs, yellow for Tourists, and white for Jews. I had a company car, a Seat Ibiza, with a tourist plate. On the day I was invited for supper in Tulkarm, Adnan had gone on ahead as it was his day off. Samir, another waiter came with me in my car. We got to the road to Tulkarm, which led off to our right. And there was a police and then an army road block. It was a military coup! I panicked. I drove straight past them, staying on the main road. Samir gave me instructions and we went down a cart track, we were going to Tulkarm, cross country. I let him drive and he kept the sidelights on to let locals know that we were friends. We seemed to go for miles through plantations, allotments and fields before arriving to a monster crowd in Tulkarm. It was like a scene from the bible, hundreds of people dressed in Jalabas with the hoods up. Adnan had arranged it to shield my car in case there were any Israeli soldiers about. I had a lovely meal with his family but was perturbed by the bareness of the house, no ornaments, no photos, nothing to make it a family home. I asked Adnan, he told me that everything that was precious was buried in the garden as Israeli soldiers were known to break into houses and smash the place up. The gravity of how stupid I had been coming to Tulkarm during a coup hit me in the face when I went to leave. There were a group of men with Israeli combats on surrounding my car. At first I thought that I had been rumbled, then they turned round and each one had a skull and cross bones painted in white on their backs. It was Adnan's friends had come to escort us back into Israel.

I got even more shocks on the way back, there were burned out cars still in flames at the side of the road and large rocks strewn over the road. All I could repeat to myself was, "You idiot!!!" I am glad that I did it though. I couldn't talk about it when I got back to the Blue Bay, in fact I couldn't voice what I had done until I was sailing from Haifa to Cyprus a few weeks later, en route to my summer resort, I wrote the whole account down in a letter.

On my third visit to Israel, I had to go and get the reps, Phillipa and Heather, home prior to the Gulf War. All the tourists had gone and there was just the accounts to tie up and get away. We decided to have some fun. We were disgusted that we as Gentiles were not issued with gas masks, we had brought thousands of pounds worth of tourism to the country but they weren't going to save our heads. Anyway, we went up to the Golan Heights to a water park in one of the hotels we used. There were wave pools and slides and everything else you would expect. We had a nice relaxing day but we noticed that nobody was using the white slide in the distance, so we went to investigate. There was a twenty-five- to thirty-foot-high slide with a ladder, as you came off the top of the slide, within about three feet, you hit a drop, straight down, of about twenty feet before the slide goes off at a right angle, towards a tiny pool of about twelve foot long. It looked absolutely fearsome and even worse when Heather and I climbed the ladder to see it from the top. Heather said, "Right Potts, I'll do it if you do." I had to take the challenge. She went first. The scream she let out as she dropped the twenty something feet, brought the rest of the water park running to see what the hell was going on. As Heather hit the right angle she was propelled forward towards the pool at a hell of a speed, I thought that the twelve-foot pool wasn't long enough to stop her, she was surely going to hit the wall at the end. Her impact in the water meant that she parted company with her bikini bottoms. The audience, who had all come running to see what the scream was all about, loved it. As she regained composure, she announced to us all, "Fucking brilliant!"

Mmmmm, my turn now. I was weak in the stomach as I climbed the ladder. I did not want to do it, but I wasn't going to be shown up by a girl. I slid off the top of that bloody slide and the scream was totally involuntary. I hit the water with a bang but managed to retain my trunks. It was absolutely out of the question to have another go. Never in a million years!

Before we left Israel, I arranged with Josi in the Ofakim office that we could go down to Eilat on the Red Sea for the weekend as thanks for all the reps hard work in the summer. He arranged for us to stay in the Penthouse Suite at Shulamit Gardens Hotel. It was brilliant, free booze, free movies, and free water sports. We took Heather's Finnish boyfriend, Arrow with us. We had an absolutely amazing time.

The drive down there was a pure delight in itself, through the Negev Desert, it was like driving through a set for a cowboy film. We learned later that there had been a number of cowboy films made there.

We went scuba diving in the Red Sea, an experience that you all have to do in this lifetime. Heather and Arrow were experienced so they went off with one instructor whilst Phillipa and I went with another. As we waded into the sea from the beach, I was amazed to find that there were multi coloured fishes swimming around our legs, in an assortment of sizes ranging from a few inches long to about a foot or more. When we got down it was like a goldfish's eye view of life underwater. There were reefs of coral with every colour and breed of fish imaginable. I panicked when a Tiger Barb flew at me and started to bite at my wet suit. It was only about four inches long but is sure gave me a fright. You can't shout out in a diving mask. There was one big wall of coral and I saw Arrow there but not Heather. I put my thumb up to him which is a bit naughty as it means you need to surface in scuba diving terms. Later by the pool when we were recounting the experience, Heather asked me if I had enjoyed her touching me up under water. I assured her that I hadn't even seen her down there, let alone felt her touch me. So God knows who the bloke was that got goosed underwater, he must have thought it was his lucky day.

Later we went water skiing and I had the most amazing experience. Whilst whizzing along on the skis, the flying fish leap across them. It was a remarkable experience.

Thassos

Thassos is the most northern of all the Greek Island close to where mainland Greece meets Turkey. The nearest Airport is Kavalla, on the mainland, and then a ferry trip over to Thassos. The journey from Kavalla to the ferry port is beautiful and the most outstanding point to note en route is the enormous storks' nests on the chimneys of the houses. The short ferry trip across to Limnes is pretty uneventful, but arrival in Thassos, you are met with an extremely pretty little island. I worked down in Limenaria at the south of the island, about half an hour's drive. The journey was spectacular, the mountain road winds for miles and you can see across to the mainland. The sea at one point changes from deep sapphire blue to aquamarine green. Then you arrive in Limenaria, a one-horse town with old-fashioned houses and tavernas. Old rusty ships moored just off shore and a dull and lifeless beach. Peak season it is ok but at the beginning and end of the season you feel like you have been abandoned in a time warp.

I was head rep and had two reps working with me, Sarah and Sarah. Confusing! So as one Sarah was blonde and English, we called her Sarah White, the other was Australian and wore thick black eye liner, so we called her Sarah Black. Then there was a Lancaster Holidays rep, Karen who was Scottish, who we nicknamed Haggis, but we sharp changed this to Shaggis when we really got to know her better.

We all lived in an apartment just behind the seafront close to Plus Minus Bar, in a quiet little cul de sac surrounded by Greek Families. It was a lovely setting and we all got on well with the Greek families. Anna our landlady lived upstairs above our apartment. She was a force to be reckoned with. Loud and brash with the best moustache describes her perfectly. She was the boss in her house and spent the days screaming at her mild-mannered husband and her daughter Despina. Anna was often down the village in her cheap cotton dress, a cowboy hat and her toothless smile. I used to call her "Toothless and Ruthless" to her face but as she didn't speak English so I got away with it.

Sarah White had been on the island the year before and had a boyfriend, Vassilis. She was from Surrey and spoke the queens English. All well and good but she had to speak Greek too and she did it in the same accent. We cried laughing. Yassoo, Ti Kanis (Hello, how are you?) became Yarsoo, ti karnis. It was hilarious. Sarah Black was batty as a fruitcake and had spent a long time in Turkey. The girls caught her one day having a shower with her shoes on. We all used to go down the beach together during siesta (midday to mid-afternoon). It was well into the season when Shaggis and Sarah White and myself had a discussion as to why Sarah Black never went topless along with the other girls. Well, I took the bull between the horns and ripped off her bikini top that afternoon on the beach. I wish I hadn't! She had thick black hairs growing around her nipples, looking for all the world like a black starfish. I was totally embarrassed, as was she. I'll never ever do that again.

The agent on Thassos was Dennis Georgis, a great big honey monster of a man, and his wife Betty who was beautiful with jet black hair and big blue eyes. Their company was 'Blue City Tours', I promptly changed that to Blue Shitty Tours. He used the local busses for excursions and airport transfers. Don't forget that the island was primitive, so the busses added an air of cheap and chatty to the overall ambiance. The Greek Night and the Reps Night were mortally embarrassing as it was all forced entertainment with local produce to eat and drink. We had an office behind their Taverna (run by Betty) on the seafront in Limenaria. It was small but adequate but there was a Greek family living above it. Well, the mother used to shriek at her seven-year-old son. Dimitri, ella na fame! (Dimitri, come and eat.) She shrieked all day long and we used to mimic her from the office. It was hilarious.

There was a Greek girl working in the office called Feni, and me being me, rhymed her name with cavla meni (horny). She was Feni cavla meni for the whole season. I must point out to all the English folks reading this, especially if you are Tutt Tutt Tutting about the last sentence, there is only the English in this world who would have a problem with that. The Greeks love that type of humour, men and women alike. Feni loved it.

It was a very short season, May to September, in Thassos as the island is so far north that they don't get the Greek sunshine for as long as the more southerly islands. We had a great season with the local Greeks, going to the local discos and Bouzouki bars. Shaggis got to know them a lot better than we did. :-)) We all were like family with the locals so it made for a very enjoyable season. Shaggis and I would spend a lot of time in the Plus Minus Bar on the corner listening to Fleetwood Mac and a chin wag with the bar owner who was a local footballer. By far the best nights were when we stole Dennis' Pajero Jeep and go out cruising around the island. Music blaring, we would head off to the other resorts. I had a car but it didn't have the pulling power of the Pajero!

Agadir Morocco

I went to Agadir in Morocco for seven weeks during the winter of 1985/6. What an experience that was. I was taking over the resort from Julia who had worked with me in Crete the previous summer. Unfortunately, there was to be no handover, she left on the plane I arrived on. Sink or swim, here we go again! Agadia Airport is just outside town and is extremely primitive, more like a cattle shed in the middle of a field than an airport. I was collected and taken to the Agents office in town where I met my co-worker/colleague, Nada. She was from Yugoslavia and the best way to describe the first meeting was "hate at first sight". She was about mid-thirties, frumpy, portly, no personality, was rude in the extreme, and pig ugly to boot. I honestly could not find one redeeming feature in the whole seven weeks we worked together. She made every task hard work. It was as if she had all-year-round PMT. She worked for Global which was part of the same group as me but honestly, If I arrived in a resort and found THAT greeting me at the airport I would get back on the plane and fly home.

I got sat in the office and found a note from Vivien who had worked in Crete with me, it said, meet me at the Dunes D'or Hotel at 5.30pm. She was doing a welcome meeting and it was invaluable to me to learn about Agadir and the excursions available. Plus, Dunes D'or was one of my hotels too. She taught me all the ins and outs in one fell swoop.

That night we went with the gorgeous Nada (which means "nothing" in Spanish) to El Rashid Restaurant on Ave Hassan II for supper. As we were walking along Hassan II, I copped an eyeful of something going on in a white van parked at the side of the road. "What the hell is he doing?" I asked Vivien.

"Probably wanking," she replied, as if it was completely normal. He was bashing the bishop in a public place on the main street. Bazaar! I found out in the following weeks just how commonplace it was. We had a nice meal at El Rashid and it was made more bearable, or it was livened up because Miss Personality Plus, Nada, went to the toilet. Unfortunately, the ladies' toilet was at the back of the gents and women had to walk down through the urinals behind men standing peeing. Well, her face was like thunder when she got back to the table. I laughed until I cried. Serves the frumpy old bitch right!

Agadir town is bordered by the sea and flanked by the mountains to the north. It is a very modern town with diagonal roads which made it easy to find your way round. Our office was halfway between the town and Avenue Hassan II, the main street. My accommodation was just about 250 yards from the office and I had to walk past little coffee shops and bars en route to work so I hardly ever cooked in the apartment. My first day in resort was a Saturday and the City Tour was my first trip. The Moroccan guide was very friendly and took time to point out places as we passed. He was invaluable. He invited me to his family home for supper that night. I felt honoured, only 24 hours in Morocco and here I was going to see how the locals lived. He picked me up on his moped after I had done my hotel duties and took me to his house. His family were fishermen. I left my shoes at the door, as is the custom and was taken in to meet his extended family, there were about three generations living in the same house. I was made extremely welcome.

The kitchen of the house where his mother and aunts were preparing the meal was extremely primitive and I was a little shocked at the way they were preparing the fish. I am not really a fussy eater but I do draw the line at anything still having its head in place staring at me from my plate. One fish had been chopped three or four times along its back, placed in a clay pot (Tajeen) and was cooking over a candle!

So the meal itself was a bit of a disaster, I ate only bread and salad. The rest of the family ate with their hands, as is the custom. We were sat on cushions in the most luxurious living room with beautiful carpets. The walls had a box like structure around three sides to sit on and a very dated sideboard at the far end. After supper everyone disappeared and left the guide and I in the room. he lit a spliff and offered me a draw. What a mistake that was! I only had a couple of draws on it and the sideboard at the end of the room with a small radio playing on it, seemed to disappear about 40 yards away. The whole room became spacial. I remember feeling that I had been anaesthetised. I have never tripped like that before nor after. I ended up sleeping in my uniform on the floor of this beautiful room and how I got up the next morning at 5am to get on the tour bus to Marrakesh I do not know.

Marrakesh to me was a big disappointment. Lovely city etc but I came back to the tour bus early and sat and broke my heart at the cruelty I had seen in the Souk. Donkeys pulling enormous loads, some with festering sores on their knees where they had fallen down and hordes of flies baying for the fester. The loads these poor animals had to carry or pull was cruelty to the extreme. Their dull lifeless eyes told volumes of the drudgery they had to endure. I saw horses and donkeys who hadn't had their bridles off for years and the skin was growing over the leather. I never want to go back.

I settled in very quickly and I was given a Citroen 2CV as my company car. I was driving down a dual carriageway one day, on my way to work when I spotted a black man on a bike, he had the biggest afro frizz but it was bright ginger, that orange kind of ginger. I nearly crashed the car into the central reservation trying to get a better look.

Days off in Agadir were taken just north on the beaches surrounding the banana plantations. Vivien and I would disappear and fall asleep with our Sony Walkmans on, only to wake up with herds of camels, goats and sheep surrounding us. One day we decided to go south to the start of the Sahara Desert. We drove for miles, past the large herds of camels and Berber settlements, and then turned along a bumpy track that took us to the sea. We passed an oasis with palm trees and wild flamingos and eventually came to the most glorious long sandy beach with rolling waves, and not a soul in sight. It went on for miles and miles. We had a walk and then settled down by some sand dunes to sunbathe. Now Paul Daniels couldn't do the trick that came next. The minute we were getting changed, there at the top of the sand dune was a Moroccan Man wanking. He seemed to appear out of thin air. We just ignored him and settled down for a rest.

We looked after guests in a five-star hotel called Les Almohades, they were all snobs. Now I have a particular intolerance of this type of person, something about the holier than thou, privileged upbringing but out of touch with reality, middle class twerps. I call them "fuckwits", and try as I might, I cannot begin to see things from their perspective. New money rattles me the most, old money is far better. One came up to me on duty one evening and in a very stern voice announced that he had mosquitoes in his room and he didn't think that a five-star hotel should have mosquitoes. I looked him straight in the face and announced, "I very much doubt that the mosquitoes know the difference between a five star and a two-star hotel." He went away with a thunderous look on his face.

Another Almohades guest was a German and his family and he was due to fly home on the first flight out. I can't remember if it was the Gatwick or the Manchester, but it doesn't matter as both flights depart within an hour of each other and the airport is only one mile out of town. I arrived at Almohades at the specified time to find they weren't there. I left them a note to say that they could either get a taxi to the airport or wait until I come back with the bus for the second flight. Well, you should have heard the abuse when I got back with the coach. He said he had been waiting at the specified time for the first coach. I told him that there were other guests from his hotel who managed to get on the coach alright. He gave me earache all the way to the airport and proceeded to hound me in the airport whilst I was organising the people on the second flight. Everywhere I went he was there behind my right shoulder. I went behind the check in desk to get away from him and also to check that his seats were still available. Vivien was there and heard the shit I was getting off him. I got him checked in and handed him his tickets and boarding passes and as he was walking away, I called him a "schwulle", which is a very rude way of telling a German that he is gay. He heard me and I didn't give a shit. So when the complaint letter came from the UK a couple of weeks later, I explained that a passenger was asking me for any free seats and I said it was "full" so the German man must have misheard me.

We had a massive problem with Germans in the Sud Bahia Hotel in the centre of Agadir. The hotel was built in a quadrant with the swimming pool in the middle. The Germans would get up first and put their towels on the sun beds to claim them for the day. My English guests would all be moaning that they couldn't get a bed. I told them, to remove the towels and claim the bed for themselves. But the lily-livered lot wouldn't do that. So I showed them the ropes. I went round at 7-30 one morning and took all the towels off the beds and put them in the pool, as they all sat eating their breakfast and watched through the windows. There was hell on. The hotel manager wasn't very pleased with me, as weren't the Germans. I didn't care, they should have had a payment scheme or a fairer system to ensure that everyone had a fair crack of the whip.

We received a telex in the office that we had a celebrity arriving in resort and asking for me to take special care of him. It was the comedian Stanley Baxter. I was a bit naughty at the airport when he arrived, his male travelling companion came up to me, on arrival, and gave the names and I told him directions to the waiting coach. The look of utter amazement and disappointment on his face was worth a giggle. I eventually said, "No, I am joking, you have a taxi to take you to your accommodation." A look of relief came over his face. That night we had a birthday party in Festival Restaurant for William, one of the Thomson reps. We had a large round table in the centre of the restaurant and being extrovert reps, we were a bit loud. Imagine my face when I regaled the story of meeting Stanley Baxter at the airport, the other reps looked mortified. He and his travelling companion were only sitting on the table behind me, listening to the whole conversation! Ooops!

I loved Agadir and the culture of the Moroccans. Lovely warm people with kind hearts. They don't drink and live their lives for their families. The places I visited were amazing, Immouser and the water falls, the start of the Sahara Dessert and the Berber tribes, Essaooira the walled city with beautiful handcrafted wooden boxes. I rode a camel, enjoyed a Moroccan meal, or two, with tribal dancers which was absolutely brilliant. The shrill scream that the women do whilst wagging their tongue will stay with me forever.

Chapter 11

Holidays, Gambia

Working for Intasun, as part of our remuneration, we would get £500 off any brochure holiday plus 15 percent. So long haul holidays were cheap as chips for us to go on. My first holiday was to Gambia to a hotel called Senegambia Beach, close to Banjul. I have always had an obsession with black culture and music. I took a friend of mine Chris, with me, and we met a few other reps there so we had quite a crowd. I didn't have much time to read up on the place before I went but all the way there, I was dreaming of long sweeping golden beaches and coffee coloured people. What a culture shock when we got off the plane, I have never neither seen nor imagined people so BLACK!! They were black as coal. It didn't bother me as I am blessed with the ability to see the person not the colour. It was a hard task on an evening outside the hotel trying to see these people in the dark. The local bar we went to was the nearest thing I have encountered to being blind. You could hear all the voices in the bar but due to very little light you had no idea where they were coming from.

The weather wasn't that good whilst we were there but we didn't care. We threw ourselves at the excursions to see as much of Africa as we could. We took a boat trip up the river

Gambia, on the ROOTS trail, to see where they took the slaves from to take to America. I had read the book Roots, by Alex Haley, and seen the TV series which was very sad. We went onto the island to the holding fort where they kept the poor unfortunates before they sailed to USA. I found a bit of clay pipe on the beach and kept it as a reminder of this sad place. We went to Kuntakinte's village and met his descendants. I was tickled by the village policeman standing with his big stick, wearing nothing but a jumper that didn't hide his bits. He had a conical piece of something over his willy and this was held up by a piece of string around his neck. Imagine a British bobby chasing you with his dick out, there would be an outcry. I loved this boat trip, we had dolphins following us all the way up the river. The funniest part was I needed the toilet, a griping pain told me so. I found my way downstairs to the ships loo and set about doing my business. There was a large pot hole next to the loo and I could see the passing countryside. Well, I must have been busy at one point and I glanced at the window to see ALL the other passengers walking down the steps right outside my porthole. I am not the sort to get embarrassed but for decency sake, I got into the crash position as you would on an airplane. Try it, you can't breathe. I was choking for breath and laughing at the same time. Hilarious!

Chris and I were mad to go on Safari but Gambia is too far north for large game. We went to the next best thing, a safari on foot along a marked trail. It was brilliant; we saw wild monkeys, termite mounds, crocodiles, peculiar wading birds. In the centre we came to a pen full of hyenas, I wasn't so keen on them. I took photo after photo but they all could not reflect the image of being there amongst it. Imagine our dismay at the end of the trail we found a signpost thanking us for our visit and announcing that in the ten years that they had been open, they had only lost one tourist to a Boa Constrictor. "Charming!"

In Gambia, I had an overbearing feeling that I had been there before. Imagine my complete surprise when I Googled my name and found that there had been a slave trader with my name. How spooky!

We went to a tribal night of dancing and eating food prepared in a traditional way, over a fire in a clay pot. It was absolutely brilliant. The dancing was phenomenal, the palm wine extremely strong and the food was delicious. Muggins here held the Black mamba snake that they brought round. They gave me a raggy bit of multicoloured cloth to hold first as a charm to stop the snake from biting me. I was well aware that it was THE most poisonous snake in Africa. I held it and had my picture taken. I don't think I would have bothered if it hadn't been for the Palm Wine.

India

I had decided to go to India for three weeks on my free holiday at the end of the first season in Rhodes and asked Kevin to come along. He only had to pay his insurance and the price of the holiday was covered with my entitlement. I chose beach bungalows in Goa, just outside Panjim for week one and three and the middle week on the North India Tour, staying in five-star hotels, visiting Agra, Jaiphur and Delhi.

The trip got off to a bad start at Gatwick Airport, we boarded the plane and got sat down and it started. The couple behind us had a Rug Rat, a toddler, a little shit of a sprog, who insisted on rattling our chairs, tugging on the head rests backwards and forwards, and the parents making absolutely no effort to control him. I was livid and we hadn't even taken off yet. I turned round and told them that if they didn't keep "THAT" quiet, I would do it for them. It is beyond me why they would take a two-year-old child on an eleven-hour flight. Don't get me wrong, I love kids normally but not when I had just finished a busy season in Rhodes and was looking forward to some relaxation. They must have rung the bell for the stewardess as we got asked if we wanted to move to two seats at the back of the plane, and we welcomed it and managed to sleep for the rest of the journey.

The bungalow was a two-storey affair with ample furniture and a ceiling fan which was a godsend. We were upstairs with a lovely view across the private beach and lovely gardens. Breakfast was al fresco across the garden close to Reception. We had an extremely relaxing stay which is more than we could say for the other reps staying in a nearby hotel, which was noisy and overcrowded. The area between our bungalows and the hotel was rural to say the least. Pigs, goats, cows and chickens running all over the roads. There was a Portuguese restaurant along from our bungalow but that was a bit of a culture shock. For those of you who enjoy Indian food, when you get there it is absolutely nothing like what you get when you are there. Chicken is on the bone and it is apparent that the poor dead creature led a very spartan life. You have to scrat for the tiniest bit of meat on each carcass. Don't get me wrong, it was tasty but nowhere near enough of it. Breakfast at the Bungalows was ample so I took to having tea and date and walnut cake on the beach on an afternoon. Very English I know but it had to keep me full.

We had a great time even though I was violently ill with the Deli Belly on our second week on the North India Tour. I had a satchel with me that was packed with toilet paper and it went everywhere with us. By this time a couple more reps had arrived. Jenny and Laura, two good friends of mine, swelling our numbers to about ten. We went to meet them at the airport on their arrival. Laura true to form walked out of the airport and announced that she was so excited that she could piss herself! We gave them the low down on the area and we all went about together. The North India Tour was a hoot! Travelling round together and seeing the sights and the temples. The camel carts were peculiar to see as was the stacked dried cow pats at the side of the road. They were burned for cooking. I asked the Tour Guide if they were for making shit kebabs and got a very frosty answer.

The five-star hotels we stayed in were extremely luxurious and to a very high standard but it was during this week that Jenny and I got Deli Belly and it was torture. We were so weak that we crawled to the toilets on our knees. Without being crude, it was like passing oxtail soup.

Delhi was frantic with more traffic than I have ever encountered anywhere else in the world. On top of the normal cars and busses there were hundreds of bicycles, Tuk tucks (three-wheeler mopeds with a cab on the back for passengers), and cows wandering around the roads and laid in the most unusual places, like in the centre of roundabouts but laid out on the road itself. Absolute chaos but somehow it worked.

We went everywhere in the Tuk tucks and they fair raced along. A bit like being in a poor Bond Film. Our hotel was on the outskirts of the centre and thank god it was away from the noise and bustle. I discovered a temple across the road from the hotel and it was nice to pop around looking at it without a guide telling every mortal fact about it. There was a bit of a park around the temple and I was perturbed to see a couple having a passionate embrace on the grass right next to a great big white bull which was lying there too, surrounded by flies. The whole park was deserted so why there?? Maybe the sacred cow was the attraction.

Agra was a fabulous place. The Taj Mahal was the highlight of the trip. How lucky I was visiting it with the love of my life, this temple built out of love with such precision and grandeur. I loved it and cherish the photos and the memories to this day.

Jaiphur, like Delhi, was chaos too. Bikes, Tuk tucks, cars, busses, people. I think the reason I like unspoilt holidays now is the chaos of India was enough for a lifetime. I was horrified to see a bicycle hurtling towards us with what looked like, at first glance, a monkey hanging onto the cross bar. It was only when it got closer that I realised it was a child. One arm and one leg over the crossbar and hanging sideways off the ruddy thing, and my, was it travelling fast.

There was an incident in the ancient temple ruins one day. Kevin and I both needed to use the loo. We found a real one which wasn't the usual hole in the ground with a bean can full of water to wash yourself. This was a largish room with a ceramic toilet in one corner and a wash basin diagonally opposite, but no lock on the door, and no toilet paper. I went first and Kevin watched the door, then he went and I watched the door, only there was an Indian man arrived and was trying to get in. He obviously didn't speak English. I shouted in the door to Kevin that there was someone here. He didn't believe me and continued to wash his bum in the hand basin. I started laughing and was just about having a fist fight with this chap whilst trying to keep the door shut.

The third and final week back in Goa, we continued to hang around with the other reps. It was ten pounds to hire a taxi and a driver for the day, and the driver would sit all day waiting to bring us back. We tried the two main beaches, Colva Beach which was thirty miles long, south of Panjim, and we hired pushbikes to cycle along it. Idyllic eh? NOT!!! The beach is littered with sea snakes, horrible foot long, fat, black and yellow things. You had to dodge them with your bike wheels. When you went swimming you had to avoid them too as they were extremely poisonous. It was novel trying to sunbathe on the beach as you got pestered every five minutes, get your hair braided, get your horoscope read, massage. You name it, they did it!

The other beach was Calagute, north of Panjim and involved a ferry crossing, ten of us in two taxis. Calagute is where the hippies congregated in the sixties. There is nothing special about the beach, sandy with a few beach bars strewn along it but still a few hippies and weirdos walking about. It was novel to sunbathe and watch people juggling by the water front or whatever other tricks they were practicing. Jenny and I were still suffering from the Deli Trots so we had devised a method of going to the toilet in the sea. If you lay on your back in the foetal position and pull your swimming costume to one side and wait for a large rolling wave to wash over you before you let go. The water washed it all away from you. RESULT!

The journey home was great as we were all booked on the same flight. Jenny who is Greek had us in fits and we got airborne and she produced "BINDI SPOTS", the red dots that

Indian women wear on their foreheads. Jenny put one on and was instantly transformed into an Indian with her dark skin. She told us that she was going down the social when she got home and she would get a house, a corner shop and enough money for a Mercedes car. We were all in fits of laughter.

America

I went to America as a second choice of resort in 1987 after leaving Crete and going to Gibraltar for the second half of the winter season. I had wanted to go to Acapulco but had been put off it by the travel guide and other people's reports. Being a seasoned traveller, I read travel guides before going to a country as opposed to letting a travel agent persuade me where to go, as our customers did. Another life lesson was learned. ALWAYS, ALWAYS go with your first choice. I am not saying it was bad in America but it was everything I didn't want. Commercial, BIG and Blousy.

I took a good friend of mine, Barty Bailey (real name Karen). She and I have the same sense of humour so it would be great to spend time with her. We had an enormous room with queen size beds in Orlando. We hired a car which did everything for you, strapped you in with the seatbelts, regulated your speed etc. We had a Shopping Mall just across the street from the hotel but there were six lanes of traffic between us and there. So you had to walk about 750 yards up to the traffic lights, wait an age for them to change and walk 750 yards back down the other side of the road to get to the Mall. A major exercise. As I have told you and you have read in this book, I am very direct and straight to the point, I don't suffer fools gladly and I am not impressed with superficial rubbish from anyone. Well, the Americans had a treat in store. How you doing today? Along with the false smile and empty words provoked Barty and I to answer in our own fashion. My first retort in the Mall was that my father had just died and my dog had been run over (said with a very straight face). Well, the woman in the mall nearly had a heart attack. We walked away before there was any more on the subject but we kept up the offensive throughout our stay. A man in Circuit City whilst we were looking at stereos announced after hearing our accents, "Oh, you are English, I would love to go to England."

Barty replied, "You would hate it, we have dog shit all over our pavements!" America is so remarkably clean.

There was a man called Lenny staying in our hotel. He told us that he was a painter and decorator, had left his wife and come on holiday alone so we let him tag along with us. He was a big built fella, alpha male type, jet black hair and brown eyes. One day by the pool he told us that he was half Crowe Indian. I said, "Are you sure that you are not full Crow as your skinny legs are just like a crow." He took us to a brilliant place on the outskirts of Orlando to do some kayaking on a natural clear water lagoon. It was absolutely excellent. We saw snapping turtles in the wild, alligators within touching distance and packs of Racoons. This had to be the best day of the holiday.

We went to a nightclub complex called Parliament House. It was enormous and had a Motel, dance floor, restaurant, shops, coffee shop and God knows what else. Barty and I had been mooching around when we settled in the Disco, leaning against the bar. I said to her that this place had everything but I hadn't seen a toilet. I turned around to the man behind me and asked where the toilet was. He pointed to an obscure door in the background and off I went. On my return, Barty was in fits of laughter and couldn't wait to tell me. The guy who had directed me to the loo had turned to her after I went and said, "I got such a shock when he said toilet, we call it the bathroom or the john." Barty then told him that he should come to Yorkshire, where we are from we call it the shithouse! He was our pal for the rest of the night. His pals were chuffed to have made some English friends and we had quite a pleasant evening with them. I remember one of them looking me straight in the eye and announcing, "My God, you just come straight out with it," and I think I had said FK or some other profanity.

We did the Disneyland trip and saw all the sights, did the rides and met Minnie Mouse. Space Mountain was right up my street. Small World had me blubbing like a baby, it was so beautiful. We watched the Grand Parade on Main Street and it really was spectacular. BUT… this is not my idea of a holiday. Even Universal Studios, Cape Canaveral and SeaWorld had little attraction. So we got in the car and headed off to Fort Lauderdale. We eventually got there. You are only allowed to do 55 MPH on the motorway. It's like driving in slow motion, it puts you to sleep. Barty had a friend from London called Joe who was from Fort Lauderdale and she was hoping to meet up with him. She phoned and phoned but couldn't get an answer so we set off to the Everglades. Notice I am saying little about Fort Lauderdale, there's nothing there, a beach, some '30s' style apartments and some palm trees and that's it! Not worth the journey really but the next bit was to be my highlight and so it was en route so to speak.

I dreamed of getting on an airboat and surfing around the Everglades and wildlife spotting. We saw plenty of Alligators in the brooks at the side of the road as we travelled down but nothing would beat seeing them from the air boat or so I thought. Barty told me that she couldn't afford it. I was gutted but not prepared to pay for her as well. She was getting a free holiday on my concession. What had transpired was that as she hadn't been able to see Joe it had ruined her holiday for her. She went into hibernation in the hotel and I started going out on my own. Imagine my fury when we got home and I recounted the episode to her sister Sue, who in turn told me that Barty had just inherited £100K from her grandmother. Women, you can keep them!

I have to write a bit about the food in America. It's cheap and thrust at you in massive quantities. Everything tastes sweet, even the meat. Breakfast in the hotel was a buffet and if you saw the amounts folk were tucking into it was disgusting. I hated it. Having spent all summer in Crete eating Greek food I was looking forward to eating bacon and eggs etc. How wrong I was, the bacon tasted sweet. There was every kind of breakfast on display and including pancakes with maple syrup. Toast and jam was all I could manage. We went to a few Diners and these were marginally better but with the disadvantage of the preying waitresses. They don't get paid enough and rely on tips to boost up their wages. So the overfriendly shit and drivel is pumped up to full volume. I hated it.

There were morbidly obese folks all over the place, MONSTERS! We were making our way out of Disney Land one evening when I spotted BIG BERTHA on a bench. Her belly was so big it hung like a curtain below the edge of the front of the seat. She was slurping on the biggest ice cream you have ever seen. "I don't know how you f**ing dare," I said as I walked past her. (By the way, I was only 11 stone then.)

Barbados

After my second season in Rhodes when Kevin ran out on me, I decided to go to Barbados. It had always been a dream of mine, me in the Caribbean. I took a Greek friend Ersan with me. Actually, he is half-Greek and half-Turkish. It was brilliant. We got an apartment on Rockley Beach at the south of the island. The balcony overlooked the beach. From the moment you arrive in Barbados the first thing you notice is the light. The place is swathed in blue tinged sunlight that is peculiar to the Caribbean and gives the place a lovely warm glowing friendly feel. The temperature all year round is in the early '60s, but we had arrived in the rainy season, November. It hardly bothered us as if it did rain it was for half an hour and that was it!

We threw ourselves at the holiday with abandon, unlike the other British tourists who had arrived with us, they were huddled in the hotel bar all night, frightened as there were a few Rasta men about. St Lawrence Gap was the next resort along from us and we would get the Reggae Bus along there on an evening. The Reggae Bus is a mini bus used as a normal bus but they are always packed and blasting out reggae music as they go. It was 2 dollars to go any distance. The bars and nightclubs were second to none. We paid 9 dollars (about £4.50) to get into The Ship Inn and got 3 free drinks thrown in. Live Reggae Bands every night and the place was rocking. There is nothing like Reggae music to make you feel good but there was also the added advantage that the whole of the bar and staff were dancing to it too. I have always loved reggae but this was out of this world. We made a few friends and learned that at five to twelve the last Reggae Bus went to Bridgetown where there was a disco on the beach called Harbour Lights. It was excellent dancing on the beach under the palm trees to brilliant reggae music. Mind you, half of the enjoyment for me was watching the blacks dance. They were excellent. We would roll back to the apartment at 2 or 3 in the morning, drag ourselves down the beach to sleep it off and sunbathe for the day and go out and do it all again the following night.

Barbados itself is very low key. Small houses and hotels, very few over two storeys high. The chattel houses painted in every colour imaginable. The small shopping malls with individual boutiques and restaurants. This was my ideal holiday!

The beautiful clean beaches with large rolling waves and the steel band playing live at the back of the beach. Absolute heaven! You could eat at most of the restaurants for around 6 dollars (£3). The local delicacy is flying fish but I am not one for eating fish with the head on so I passed on that. I love fish otherwise. The food is beautiful, fresh and appetising.

I decided to go and discover more of the island and made my way into Bridgetown, leaving Ersan on the beach. I found a submarine that would take you down for 30 dollars. I had only just learned to scuba dive in Rhodes that year but didn't have a PADDI license so couldn't do it here. The trip under the sea was amazing, we saw shipwrecks and coral reefs and amazing wildlife. I was still buzzing from that trip when I walked across the car park and found a helicopter doing Island Tours for another 30 dollars, so off I went. I have a passion for helicopters and can't get enough of the rush as the machine whisks you off the ground up into the sky. We flew over the famous cricket ground, the race course and the rest of the island but the highlight for me was over the sea where you could see all the shipwrecks lying there at the bottom of the ocean. What a brilliant day!

Ersan and I had a bit of a fall out as he had picked up this woman on the beach. She was pig ugly, had hairy nipples and bossy to boot! She only wanted to go where she wanted to go, we had no say. In my book, if we are paying, then we call the shots. If we wanted to eat prawns then she wanted burgers and I was bloody sick to death of her. So I left them to it. I have a sixth sense about people and she rattled my nerves far too much for me to associate with her. Well, she ended up stealing all of Ersan's money and serves him right. The worst bit was that Ersan blamed the lovely maid who cleaned our room. I was mortified for her and went to see the manager myself to explain the situation. It was during this rift with Ersan that I went for a walk up the beach towards Bridgetown to clear my head and get a bit of space. I was amazed that I hadn't gone very far when I stumbled on the Hilton Hotel. It was on the beach and had its own beach bar. I got talking to some English folk at the bar and discovered that they were British Airways cabin crew on a stopover. So I had a very pleasant afternoon with them chatting about the perils of tourism and getting quietly plastered.

I had become friendly with a rich Arab lad, Peter, whose father had string of racehorses on the island. He drove a Delorean and I was scooting about with him all over the place. There is no better way to see a place than with a local. I had a great time whilst Ersan entertained the bitch and wasted his money. Peter's friend Stephen worked for American Airlines and we became good friends also. I went to Bridgetown one night with these two and had my first taste of an all-black club.

Well, words cannot describe the atmosphere, it was dark, it was sleazy, it was highly charged sexually and the slow reggae music was just out of this world. I dance like most westerners and keep the beat. Here they were keeping some obscure beat and working their bodies together in an extremely sexual manner. Almost like tantric sex. I have never been so turned on in my entire life. We didn't stay too long as my heart couldn't stand the strain.

Now I am not one to boast about sexual encounters but a very funny incident occurred on Rockley Beach a couple of days after we arrived. Ersan and I had gone for a walk up the beach at about 6pm, which is around sunset. We collected pieces of coral and shells and the usual beach holiday pastimes, when a black lad appeared from nowhere. Ersan had walked a bit ahead so I talked to this lad who was about 18 and called Trevor. He made it clear that he was looking for sex and asked what the relationship was with Ersan and I, and were we gay. I explained that I was but he wasn't. Now my curiosity and the stories about black men being bigger and better got the better of me and I went into the bushes with him. Well, truth to tell, he pulled out the biggest, blackest, erect dick I have ever seen. I straight away said, "What do you want me to do with that, dance around it?" It was like a bloody Maypole. So I left him to sort himself out and rushed along the beach to Ersan.

The last day in resort was a very sombre affair. Neither of us wanted to leave. I was in the depths of despair and depression. We went into Bridgetown to get some shopping and came back to the reception in the apartments at the designated time to get picked up to go to the airport. At this point I will tell you that Ersan and I only spoke Greek to each other when in the company of the other English in the Apartments as we didn't want to get embroiled with them. Imagine their surprise when the Rep arrived and told us that there was a 24-hour delay on the flight and they were putting us up in a five-star hotel down at Silver Sands for the night on full board. We both looked at each other and said, "F**king brilliant."

We got some extremely peculiar looks from the other English who had sat it out all holiday in the bar at the Apartments, fearful of the Rasta Men out in the street and whingeing that the bar staff were speaking Patwa.

Silver Sands was idyllic, a welcome rest from all the partying. We sat on the lawn drinking cocktails and watching the humming birds. Another day in Paradise!

Ersan missed his connecting flight to Amsterdam so had to butter up the staff at Gatwick to get uploaded onto another flight.

They say that god works in mysterious ways but this was amazing. My friend Sue had done her summer season in Thailand and had just arrived back in the UK as I got back from Barbados. Of course I was ranting about Barbados and how brilliant it was when Sue suggested that we should go on her concession. WHAT! Barbados twice for FREE! I had no hesitation. We booked and we went. This time we took along with us Matthew and Tony who had been Sue's reps in Thailand. Tony was a real Jack the Lad but Matthew was a drip. A right mother hen. We got booked in an apartment in

Holetown, the only one we could get, but miles away from Rockley beach. We hated it. Nothing to keep us there so we asked the rep to move us ASAP! To top it all when we arrived at the Airport in Barbados and collected our luggage, mine was covered in fuel which had seeped through to the contents. I had about a dozen Polo Shirts, Lacoste of course, £1 each from Turkey. They had all changed colours and were a right mess. MMMM Insurance claim would offset the second holiday costs.

On the first night I rang Peter the Arab and he picked us up and took us out in St Lawrence Gap. We all agreed that we would be better off at that end of the island. So we got transferred to the Magic Isle apartments, right on the beach at Rockley Beach. Two twin bedrooms, straight through the gardens and onto the beach. Perfect. I shared with Sue whilst the boys were in together. We had a right laugh. Sunbathing during the day and partying at night. I told a Rasta man Mark on the beach that Sue fancied him and he wouldn't leave her alone. We used to send Matthew up to the Mall for frozen yoghurts, they were like ice cream but far more yummy. The steel band was playing every day at the back of the beach and life was perfect. Sue and I would people watch from our sun beds. There was a very ugly black man who would prowl up the breach in very skimpy Speedos (Americans call Speedos Banana Hammocks) and no kidding, his dick went from the front right 'round to the side, what a banana! It was amazing! But we never once saw him cop off. We joked that the wedding tackle wasn't the best attracter.

Tony was the adopted stud at the Hilton Hotel and would disappear up there to service the Cabin Crew. He was a good-looking lad but what got us was that he would roll down the beach the next day, un showered, and lie in the sun all day, stinking and he never once went for a swim. Dirty little bugga!

Tony and I decided that we would smoke a joint before going out one night. Neither of us knew how to roll one so we had to buy one ready rolled off Mark on the beach. Two policemen stood and watched as Mark rolled them and took our money. Bizarre!

We smoked it in the apartment before getting a taxi along to St Lawrence Gap. My head was in pieces. I must have had a smile a mile wide on my face and I could hardly stand up. Everything was funny. I'd look at Tony and we would fall about laughing. In the Ship Inn the music was banging out and with our heightened senses it was twice the fun. The British Cricket Team were in there and at one point someone said I was dancing next to Gladstone Small but I hadn't a clue who he was. He didn't even look familiar.

Sue copped off with a Swedish lad on the beach early on in the holiday but halfway through she met the man of her dreams. In between times we had befriended two American lads. Mike and Clyde. They were real hillbillies. Trying to show us card tricks in a nightclub. DUH! We went around with them for a couple of days but soon got sick as they weren't the party animals that we were. One night the lads and I were along the Ship Inn and Sue had stayed at the Apartment to catch up on sleep. Mike and Clyde were there and at one point Mike asked where Sue was. SHIT I said, Sue told me to let you have the apartment key and she wants you to go and see her. I gave him the key and off he went. I cried laughing the next day when Sue told me that she awoke from a deep sleep to find Mike sitting on her bed with two cans of lager. What a hoot.

One evening when we were all getting ready to go out, Sue was in the shower and I broke in using a coin to open the lock. I proceeded to take flash photos of her and told her that I was going to sell them to Penthouse. She was screaming blue murder at me and crouched in the bottom of the shower tray. It was hilarious. I didn't tell her until later in the holiday that there was no film in the camera.

It was about halfway through the holiday that we were in Harbour Lights in Bridgetown, dancing on the beach and it was raining. I smoked at the time so I ran under cover to hand my fags to Sue who was sitting at the bar. She told me that she had someone to introduce me to. His name was Steve and he worked on Dutch millionaire's yacht as a chef. I took one look at him and told her that he was the one she would marry. They are still together to this day so where I got that from, I don't know. We got a sneaky peek at the yacht; it was out of this world. What poor Steve didn't know at the time was that she had to get rid of the Swede pretty sharpish.

Well, all good things had to come to an end and it was time to go home again. Stephen from American Airlines managed to get us the seats by the emergency exits on the plane so we knew that we would have a comfortable journey home. What transpired was embarrassing. We arrived at the airport in no hurry as we knew our seats were safe. We then found out that there was a delay. No problem we thought. We checked in and went through to the lounge. Unfortunately, the bar and cafeteria were closed. No problem we thought, but the heat was horrendous and we were all cooped up in the lounge. We sat in a far-off corner as we had had our fill of moaning tourists in our summer resorts. Suddenly there was an announcement over the tannoy, "Would Howard Potts please make his way to the American Airlines office." They were our flight handlers so I went, all the while thinking that they had better not change our seats. I got there and it was Stephen just wanted to say goodbye. Whew I thought. I went back through to the lounge and told the others. Next thing I was asked to go back again to the AA office. This time I was convinced that they were after our seats. No, Stephen had stolen the buffet from the AA flight from New York and did we want some. Well, I went back into the lounge with the biggest tray of club sandwiches, cakes, biscuits, chocolate and drinks. I was embarrassed but even more embarrassed when we got on the plane eventually and got the best seats.

Kelly, the Intasun Area Manager travelled home with us. She was in a hell of a state leaving her beloved Barbados and her boyfriend. I had known her from Costa Brava days as she had been a friend of Wanda. I heard shortly after that she had won the lottery on Barbados and had returned there. What a happy ending.

Sadly, ILG went under in 1990. Our airline, Air Europe, dragged the company into liquidation. I was sent out to Benidorm to look after the resort whilst all the resort managers, from all over the world, were at a meeting in Mallorca. I had been asked by a number of people what was happening. As usual in these situations, the staff are the last to be informed. As I am extremely intuitive, and quite able to look after myself, I went to the airport and got myself home with another Tour Operator. It was only one day earlier than planned anyway. I rang the main office the next morning to tell them that I had got back home. "Haven't you heard?" the boss asked, "The company have gone into liquidation."

"NO," I lied. He-he. What a predicament, all those poor tourists in resort, all over the world, and all the Area Managers in Mallorca. I am glad I was out of it.

The end of a very happy era!

Chapter 12

Back in the UK, London

I came back to the UK after the collapse of ILG and initially went to stay in Newcastle but there wasn't any work to be had so I moved to London to work in my brothers Travel Company. At this point I was fed up of running away and was desperate to put down some roots. Alan and Debbie had acquired a large five bed roomed house, just off the Broadway in fashionable Crouch End, near Highgate. It gave me a chance to test the waters and see if I was going to stay in the UK and it also gave me an opportunity to spend some time with Alan's son Jamie. Jamie, like Neville had been, was mad about nature so I renovated the fishpond in the garden. We went to a local pond and got duck weed and pond creatures for it, and unbeknown to us we must have scooped up some fish eggs because there were lovely fish appeared in the pond, which Jamie would catch with his bare hands.

I went mad going everywhere in London, catching up with friends, partying, and dinner parties. I met a lad called Steve who I knew only by sight in Newcastle. I was in a bar in Islington having only been in London 5 days and spotted Steve. He got a shock when I went to talk to him as he had only been in London 2 days. He was a croupier in a local casino. We painted the town red and did everything together. Bars, Clubs, Richmond by the river, you name it, we did it.

My nephew Jamie had a friend who lived around the corner called Hugo, whose mother was an Opera singer, a Soprano. Hannah became a very good friend of mine and I would babysit Hugo whenever she needed me to. I love all kinds of music but nothing has ever moved me to tears like sitting on the stairs outside Hannah's music room, in her house, listening to her having an audition for a part. I have never heard anything quite so beautiful like it and have been a huge fan of opera ever since.

I am not going to bore you with London, it was a bad move. Approximately three years I stayed there and after eight years on Greek Islands it was intolerable. I was fed up of weirdos, alternative everything, hustle and bustle, overcrowded roads, trains, busses. I think the breaking point came when I wanted to play tennis and rang to book a court, we can fit you in around six weeks' time. I might not want to play in six weeks' time. I went swimming in Islington and the pool was divided into three lanes. Learners, novices and advanced! Bloody boring swimming round like a goldfish in a bowl. GET ME OUTA HERE!!!!!

One last incident that is worth a mention. I very rarely used the underground, I preferred to drive everywhere. I was coming back to Crouch End one night on the tube when this outrageous incident occurred. The tube stopped at a station and just as the doors began to close prior to moving on, a man lunged from his seat to try and get out of the doors before they closed. Whether he was on drugs, drunk or on medication didn't really matter. The doors were nearly closed and he stumbled and hit his head and collapsed on the floor of the train. I immediately jumped up and pulled the emergency chain. Within minutes there was a Guard and a Policeman in the carriage and they actually stepped over the man on the floor and asked who pulled the emergency chain. I could not believe what was happening. I admitted to it and all the while this poor man is lying in a pool of blood. So folks, if you ever go to London, don't be public spirited as you will be accused and get the blame.

Back in the UK, North Yorkshire

I moved back to North Yorkshire in May 1994. I had intended to go and live in the cottage at Carrsides Farm but the thought of no central heating did not bode well with me having spent eight years in Greece and three years in a centrally heated flat in London. I phoned Chris Stamford Bewlay and asked if his brother's cottage in Cleasby was still free. Michael, Chris' brother, had died tragically at 27 from a brain haemorrhage. So to cut a long story short, I moved into Ivy Cottage and have been here ever since. I loved the place the moment I walked through the door for the first time. Wooden beams in the Living Room and Dining Room, a stone fireplace with open fire grate. Mind you the place was a mess as it had been unoccupied for about five years. There were cobwebs and dead flies and spiders everywhere. It took a team about 6 family members to clean it top to bottom. Madge sat downstairs and professed to be looking after Carolyn's two kids, Ben and Bronya, whilst we worked. She was to lift into the car afterwards and I was a bottle of Baileys Irish Cream down on the deal.

In the beginning I was in an extremely fragile state, I had given myself six months and if I couldn't make a go of it, I wanted out. This wasn't a threat, it was a cold hard fact. Death was preferable to… To what? I didn't know what. Life on the run was what I was used to. The answer I could not put words to was that I was going to have to face the past. Suicide was much more preferable than what I had to sort out. The following poem I wrote will summarise it better. I had been writing a joke book with a friend, Harry, and I wrote the poem so that he could begin to understand what I was going through.

Poem

Through the dark and dusky recesses of a life that has been so blue,
Through the cobwebs of a painful past, a light came shining true,
The light was pure and simple, not a facet to be seen,
Bringing forth the recognition of a life that might have been,
A welcome hand I reached out and grasped it firm and strong,
Accepting with the knowledge that it had been too long,
The poison in the brain cells, too painful to let go,
The dampened fire within my heart was going to have to show,
The passion that came flooding out, overwhelming with its heat,
Broke down the barriers of many years, myself I had to meet!
I met the challenge meekly, I didn't want to look,
Alarm bells ringing in my head all the while we wrote our book,
I had to look inside myself, I avoided like the plague,

I'd laugh and joke beyond control to keep the hurting vague,
The fight going on inside my head was turning me quite blind,
If you were the monster consuming me, why were you being so kind?
I realise now I have conquered it, in a week that has been too long,
The turmoil dissipated leaving me vulnerable but strong,
I have unloaded all my gremlins, inner anxieties and the strife,
To sum it up, I'd have to say that, I have had too much of life!
My strength comes back to me day by day, I am sleeping better too,
I am sorry that I worried you, this was nothing to do with you,
My love for you is natural, pure and true in every form,
You took me in so easily and made me feel so warm,
I recognise the potential, our friendship was meant to be,
A once in a lifetime encounter, you didn't have to look to see,
The empathy and the kinsman ship, our access to each other's brain,
The strength of our bonding, accepting without strain,
I will always be your friend, your mainstay, rod and staff,
Long may we love each other and make each other laugh.

I wrote it but the real truth was to show itself later in therapy. I struggled to find work and was sinking fast. My brother Alan offered to set me up in business and came up to see an office I had found. It was only £25 a week. Off he went back to London and that was that so I thought. I knew the job inside out having worked in London for him for nearly three years. Plain sailing from here so I thought. Then Alan rang and said that I had to go down to London. I could not see the point and knew in my heart of hearts that Debbie his wife, and a co-director of the company, wanted to get her oar in on the job. I refused to go. So I cancelled the office and it was a number of weeks later that Alan rang me, one Sunday afternoon when I had just got back from the pub. "What's happening with this office?" he asked in his usual arrogant voice. So I gave it to him, full throttle. I have only spoken to him once since that day and quite honestly, that's the way it's going to stay. Sometime during my time in Cleasby, and I cannot give a date, my mother had been contacted by a distant cousin from Billingham. He was looking into the family tree and had found her through that. The biggest revelation of my life was that Mother's grandfather, Etty's father, and his brother had come across from Ireland to find work. They had left the family farm in County Mayo as there wasn't enough to divide between the FIVE of them. Eureka! I could see it plainly now. I didn't fit in with the English, because I was Irish. It all made sense. I act like an Irish man and think like an Irish man.

This was to become more apparent years later when I met my friend Ella. She is from Dublin, a farmer's daughter and if I told you her tale you would cry your eyes out. She, like me, has seen life, lived it, had her face rubbed in it and survived, just like me. She had her 60th Birthday in a small pub near Barnard Castle. It was a fantastic night, the place was full of Irish, they had done their own catering and we danced, and listened to the "crack" and told jokes. Brilliant night! What I like about the Irish is that they are all comfortable in their own space, tell it like it is and have a brilliant sense of humour. Who does that describe? ME!! I had been to posh parties and Hunt Balls that year but nothing topped Ella's 60th.

Throughout my gloomiest moods and depressions, I never lost my sense of humour. Chris Stamford Bewlay was a medical rep and was marrying his Doctor wife, Jane. Chris and I have always looked out for each other since the George days and remain so to this day. I was an usher at his wedding and took the job seriously until a friend Sue came in and whispered a joke to me. I have to tell you the joke for you to understand better why I reacted like I did.

#What three things should you not say in a Gay Bar?
1/ Mine's a large stiff one!
2/ I'll toss you for it!
3/ Will you push my stool in!

I erupted into great guffaws of laughter and because of the seriousness of the situation, every time I remembered it, I started laughing again. Poor Chris must have thought I was completely mad.

Village life to me is much more preferable than the time I had lived in cities, Athens, London, Tel Aviv and Barcelona but in the cities at least you were anonymous. Here in the village, it's like living in a goldfish bowl, especially as my cottage is in the centre of the village green. I did try from the start to be amenable but slowly they creep in and become a nuisance. First it was expected that I give 10p a week to the church and the village hall fund, not a great amount I know but I am the one in charge of my finances and I resent being told what was expected from me. Anything that is taking place in the Hall or Church means that we lose our parking places. Have you noticed that nobody can walk these days, they have to park right at the door. I had a few run ins with people in the village and decided that I can't be that petty minded so kept myself to myself. You will all of heard of village idiots well we have quite a few people vying for the post.

I live in the centre of the village green surrounded by grass and the council cut it regularly throughout the summer. When I have a party though I like to cut it myself and have it looking like a lawn. The council just leave the cuttings to die on top of the grass. On one such occasion I cut the grass and put the cuttings behind the wall at the side of the village hall next door. That night I had the head of the parish council knocking at my door informing me that there had been a complaint about it. I asked him who had complained and he could not divulge so I did a bit of snooping and found out. It was Hazel from the farm outside the village, from a different parish even. So that Sunday I made a point of being outside whilst they were going to church. "Good morning Howard," she said as she went past my house. I said, "Don't good morning me Hazel, what's this about you going to Norman about my grass clippings?"

"EEH, it wasn't me," she said. So I told her that she had been seen at Norman's door. "Well, I wasn't alone," she said.

So I told her, "One minute it wasn't you and now it was you, you are nearly sixty years old, for fuck's sake stand up for what you have done!" Her husband just gawped on in amazement. I think the vicar walked past at some point and learned some extremely coarse language.

St Lucia

My neighbours in Cleasby, Ann and Gareth have the most beautiful villa in St Lucia close to Rodney Bay, the main resort. Built into a hillside, and the only property on that hill, it looks out over the sea and you can watch the cruise liners leaving Castries, the main town. The main house of the villa becomes one with the balcony when you open the windows and shutters. A massive living space! The balcony is exceptional; one end is the dining table and chairs, two rocking chairs in the middle, and then a wicker three-piece suite at the other end. I went over for two weeks in January 2009 and then again in January 2011. I loved sitting on that balcony, reading, drinking etc and watching the humming birds enjoying the potted flowers which lined the railings. The bamboo wind chimes swaying gently in the breeze giving a slightly wooden chime. Total bliss!

It was just as enticing on a balmy evening when we came back in to sit and have a gin and tonic by candle light before going to bed. Just around the corner from the villa is Windjammer Hotel, about five minutes' walk. It has a small beach, south facing and it is beautiful to spend a day along there. There is a very small beach just down from the villa which is excellent for snorkelling and sun bathing.

St Lucia is not as tourist driven as Barbados and offers a better insight to Caribbean life. It is very laid back and low key. Rodney Bay is a large yachting marina alongside Reduit Beach and the beach road in between. The main bars and restaurants are on the beach road. The first year I was there the beach road was a teaming mix of locals and tourists and the atmosphere was brilliant, with the exception of the Americans who stood smoking cigars in the bars. Cigarettes are bearable but great big billowing clouds of heavy smoke are totally NOT!

I was a bit disappointed to find that the music was not all reggae which had been my favourite in Barbados. The bars played a mix of music and we still managed to have a good time. Lime on the Bay had live music, further along Delirious, which I nicknamed Dementia, had a German DJ who played a mix of very European music.

There is a fantastic restaurant right on the beach called Spinnakers serving an eclectic mix of Caribbean and European foods. Perfect for the start of a great night out! They even have Greek salads so I was a little bit biased. Further up the beach road there are Steak Houses, Indian and Chinese food. You name it and you can get it.

Just north of Rodney Bay is a sleepy little hamlet called Gros Islet where, on a Friday night, they close off all the roads and have a massive street party called "Jump up". Reggae music blasting in the town square, food and jewellery stalls all along the streets. The atmosphere is brilliant, everyone dancing in the street and the later you stay the better it gets. For me it was a fat boys dream tasting all the locally produced food.

We lived it "large" in St Lucia and would go to Sandals for lunch, as in we would pay for lunch and then make full use of the facilities for the rest of the day. Rolling home so pissed at the end of the day. £16 for lunch and it was buffet, eat and drink as much as you like, even have a bottle of wine each (or two). The beach there is lovely golden sand and gently shelving into the sea. I can't say enough good things about it but there is one major downside to it, AMERICANS! Well, they are a bit loud. Not all of them but it does seem like a large proportion of them fit that bill. I go on a beach to relax and read a book whereas the yanks talk incessantly. One day at Pigeon Island we sat on the beach and two Yankee women were next to us yakking, and it went on and on and on and on. We had to go for a swim to get a bit of peace. I can't tell you how many times I wanted to say, "Will you just shut your fucking gobs!" We were in swimming when these two women started to come into the water. They were so huge that I was sure that the water level was going to rise dramatically. I started to sing "Here come the girls" and we all laughed but a black man in a canoe selling Conche shells and beads thought we were laughing at him. I had to quickly and quietly tell him the story. He howled laughing too.

We did the tourist stuff like going down to see the Pitons, two large mountains rising out of the sea, a bit like two breasts. We went to the volcano crater and drove inside, parking right alongside the bubbling earth. We wanted to go in for a swim close by but the smell of sulphur was overpowering. I didn't want to walk round for the rest of the day smelling like a fart.

We stopped in a small town en route to the Pitons and being Saturday the locals were getting ready for a night out. I thought it novel to see the coloured chattel houses and the women going about their business with a head full of rollers. It was like the clock had turned back to the '50s.

A highlight for us was meeting Ami Winehouse in the Sport Hotel. We had gone for supper and later went down to the beach bar, Ami was there and we spent a very pleasant evening with her. I found her very vulnerable and we managed to have a good dance and laugh with her. I will remember as long as I live when she said to me, "Come on Howard, and teach me some Geordie." It was a bit ironic really as I have never really got into her music. It started raining when we were dancing and the marble floor became slippery and perilous. So imagine our absolute horror when we got home to the UK to pictures of that night with Ami falling on the marble and the caption, "Winehouse so pissed that she can't stand up." Nothing could have been further from the truth. Yes, we were all a bit tipsy, it was free drinks in the Beach Bar, but to twist the truth for effect was pathetic and typical of the cretins that write for the newspapers. Well, she is dead now so how do they feel now? Probably don't care as they will be slagging off some other celebrity. In my mind they are just as guilty of killing Ami as the drugs and alcohol that killed her.

Derek Fields (Lord Fields)

Derek is one of my horsey friends and has been since the early '70s. He had the most beautiful chestnut horse and being six foot five inches tall, Derek certainly looked like a lord on his back. He certainly acted it too. He had left his wife after 25 years marriage and had run off with a young man. The tiny minds in the county still bleat on about it today, forty plus years later. The bigger minds accept that he had been living a lie for 25 years and was now looking for happiness.

He has the same sense of humour as I do, but he can take things one step further than I can, resulting in me being mortally embarrassed. The best example that comes to mind is the Hunt Ball at Wynyard Hall, Derek got on the table and did a head stand in the trifle.

He rang me one day in the early '90s and asked if I wanted to be a stooge for a Hypnotist who was appearing at the Mall in Stockton. Of course I was all for it. So on the night, we arrived at the Mall, which had been a Cinema in its heyday, we were shown up to what would have been the Projection Room, now the Hospitality Suite. We were introduced to the Hypnotist, a small little man with pointy fingers. I took an instant dislike to him. He gave me the creeps. He gave us our briefing, mingle in the crowd and he would call us onto the stage. All well and good.

The stage was set with a semi-circle of chairs, and when we were called onstage, Derek got to sit on a chair somewhere near the middle, I was stood behind them, about four chairs to the left of him. We were supposed to have been "put under", when I could feel myself getting the giggles. I was very amused at some of the shenanigans the Hypnotist was having people doing. The BIG CLANGER was when he put his hand on Derek's shoulder and brought him awake. He told him that the woman standing off stage, wearing black and white, had his willy (penis) in her handbag. Derek proceeded to fight with her and try to get her handbag from her. I just bust into great big guffaws of laughter, which became more exaggerated when I saw the look of pure hate from the Hypnotist. Needless to say, I never returned upstairs for the De brief and drinks party afterwards. It was far better having a good giggle to myself for weeks afterwards when I remembered the night.

Derek's birthday was the next time we met up. He rang to invite me to a pub crawl around Middlesbrough, starting off at an Irish Bar close to the Bus Station. I arrived as planned and met him with all his pals, and as was the custom, Derek stood a round of drinks. I went to the bar to help him. There was a little old Irish man sitting at the bar, minding his own business. Derek asked him if he would like a drink, and he declined. Derek insisted by saying, "It's my birthday, let me buy you a drink!" The old man declined again. Derek then changed it to, "If you give me a kiss, I will buy you a drink!!!" I was mortified, and I think the old man was too.

The pub crawl went along nicely and we ended up in a Gay Club where there was a stripper appearing. So when the stripper did appear, who did he choose from the audience to assist him with his act? Derek and I! He was standing there on stage with a towel around his waist, and offered a bottle of baby oil each to Derek and I. I was rubbing it on his skin, whilst Derek was fighting to get his hand down the front of his towel. I honestly thought there was going to be a fight, as some strippers are straight and only out to make money. I was giggling as usual and had to leave the stage. Just as well I did because I wouldn't have missed the show for anything. The stripper was gyrating around Derek in a very suggestive fashion. Derek was loving it, but I could tell by the look on his face that he was looking for the next bit of devilment. I wasn't disappointed! The stripper laid Derek on his back and proceeded to gyrate over the top of him, only he was naked now. They got into the 69 position and the strippers willy was being gyrated around his face. Oh my God, Derek was only gyrating his face trying to get the willy in his mouth! I couldn't believe my eyes. I was crying with laughter as were the rest of the crowd. I think the stripper was getting a bit sick of his life by the end of the show.

Derek eventually got married again, this time to Steven, a fashion designer from Stockton. I had never been to a gay wedding before, and it was at Pinchinthorpe Hall, near Guisborough, so I was really looking forward to it. On the day, there were only about twenty of us including the Groom and Groom. It was a very classy affair in a very classy venue which was spoilt a bit by Steven's very unclassy brother who wanted to fight all the puffs to show how masculine, and definitely not gay, he was.

Steven was dressed all in white, in a suit that he had designed, and looked immaculate. Lord Fields was in grey as befitted the occasion. Sadly, there weren't many representatives from Derek's family there, and I know that he would have loved his daughter to have come. I was tagging along with a friend and his wife but when it came to the reception, I was sat at the table with a very striking young man, who turned out to be Derek's brother's son, his nephew. I asked him, "When did you find out that your Uncle Derek was really your aunty?" He let out a great big guffaw of laughter and said, "Funny you should say that," and went on to tell me that when he was at Naval College, his mother rang him and said that someone in the family had come out as gay, but he never in a million years would have guessed Uncle Derek.

Derek now spends a lot of his time in France at their second home and I have promised that one day I will go and visit them.

Chapter 13

Therapy

I rattled about in various jobs and could not shake off this suicidal feeling. I was totally spent and frustrated that I had to do something about it, but what? I went to the doctors and asked if I could get into therapy on the NHS. He arranged the appointments for me, six in all, and I started having an hour session a week in Richmond. My therapist was extremely good and took me through the stages after learning what the base of the problem was. Imagine my surprise when she announced on the first session that all my problems in life were to do with abandonment, starting from my stay in hospital at age five. She had worked that out from my medical records. What a revelation! All my other ailments throughout my life were related too. Stomach ulcers from stress, piles from bad eating habits etc. The light was beginning to shine. My only criticism of her would be that she asked me at one point how many sessions did I think I would need. I went into panic, I thought she didn't care either. As I sit here now, I think it was extremely foolish of her. Asking a suicidal person to assess what capacity of care it takes to make them better. She may as well have just handed me a gun and said get on with it. Throughout therapy I could never work out why I was feeling suicidal. What was it that was driving me into these thoughts of doing myself in? The truth was that I would rather have died than look at the truth I was going to have to face. The other worrying factor was, "What does this all say about me as a person?" It soon became apparent that ALL families have their bogeys in the cupboard and there wasn't a family on this earth that was normal, whatever normal is!

I went through the stages of therapy with her but she only provided the tools for what I needed to get ahead of. As a rational thinker and determined being it took me six years to work everything out in my head. There were three main areas that needed addressing. The death of my brother, and the leaving of my father, and Kevin's leaving. Then there were three sub divisions of being abandoned three times. Funnily enough I managed to sort the death of Neville out in my head by myself and can talk about it freely now, so long as no one makes any show of horror whilst I tell the tale. I have got over all the feelings of guilt and loss, BUT and even after so many years, it still pops up and surprises me in the most weird of situations. I went recently to a new Soul and Funk Club in Newcastle called Hoochie Coochie. I had been waiting to go for weeks since it opened. When the first band struck up, I just stood and blubbed my eyes out. Our Neville would have just absolutely loved it!

27 years is a long time to carry the guilt around in your head and makes it harder to be able to turn around and face it. The longer you wait, the harder it is to look. I never knew how to react when Father walked out on Christmas Eve 1976. I now know that it was because I had been abandoned in hospital when I was five and my parents not coming to see me and here were the same feelings of panic. I often imagined my

father turning up at an airport when I was working abroad. What would I say and how would I react? The truth then was that I didn't know. I dreaded the thought of it. When Alan, my brother, eventually got back in touch with him and started to tell me stories, it was as if he was talking about someone I had known in a previous life. But, when Alan rang me to tell me that Father had called him to announce that he had a new baby daughter, that WE had a sister. I was incensed. Most peculiar!

The therapist sat me down one day and started to chat. What happened next, I never saw coming. She turned the spare chair round and said, "Your father is back for a few minutes, tell him what you think." I went numb and stopped breathing. The Therapist jumped up and started thumping my arm shouting, breathe, breathe. I went into a rant like a madman, and I can tell you I never once thought the thoughts that were spilling out of my mouth. "You fucking bastard you, you ran off when we were all setting off on our careers, you hadn't the balls to turn up at Neville's funeral…" It went on and on. I was exhausted and a little embarrassed about my language. That was it, I had had it bottled up all those years and it had to come out. I walked out of that office crying but I knew that a great big black cloud had disappeared from my shoulders. Imagine the relief that 27 years of pent-up emotion was now available to put to rest.

It transpired later when relating this story about my father to my relatives that it wasn't the first time that he had run off to have an affair. When I was five and in hospital he had gone then. It took Uncle Arnold and Uncle Alan to go and get him to fetch him home. He was in Doncaster working for David Brown Tractors. So there was the reason for my lack of visits in hospital that lead to my problems with abandonment.

Mother looking after number one again, *Fuck the kids, I come first!*

The next week, we tackled Kevin. When the therapist started the session with the words, "Now let's see about this hate you have for Kevin." I argued that I loved Kevin, I didn't hate him. She suggested that I have a dinner party and make it a momentous occasion to kill Kevin off in my mind and move on. I couldn't see it working and it was years before I realised that Kevin had done exactly what my father had done. Run off in a cowardly fashion, without a word and left me in limbo land again. One trait that I had at the time was that you could tell me until you were blue in the face what the problem was but until I understood it and recognised it, I wouldn't or couldn't take it on board. I have to work it out in my head and see it plainly. I tried lots of tactics to try and get ahead of it. I went down to Ellesmere Port, on the Wirral and sat outside his mother's old house even though I knew he wasn't there. I found the address for him that was on 192.COM. I went three times to the house but could not knock on the door. I came back the next day and after two attempts, I eventually knocked on the door and a lady answered and told me that he had moved about two years previous. Back to square one. I eventually went home and found him again on 192.COM, he was living in Wallasey.

All of my close friends that knew about Kevin kept telling me to move on, well you can't move on until you are ready to. No amount of pushing can make you. You can't tell a rape victim to go out and have casual sex. Same difference. I was abandoned, it has coloured my life since age five and no amount of pushing from any source will make me set myself up for another kick in the teeth like that again. I have been single ever since and I really cannot see me having another affair unless it was someone with a great big heart or someone who has had similar experiences, or a therapist/psychiatrist!

Lots of things became clear after therapy, and remember the therapy doesn't stop just because you stop going to the sessions. Your head carries on self-analysing. I realised that Father leaving and Neville's death in my mother's eyes, only happened to her. It didn't affect us (in her mind). After therapy I was able to go to the Crematorium on the 29th September, the day he was killed, for the first time since Neville's death. Imagine my feelings when I found Mother and Ken there and she screamed accusingly, "What are you doing here?" It was as if I was intruding on her grief. Typical of her as I have said before she is a small-minded selfish bitch. I couldn't believe what she was saying. That was the beginning of the end of any relationship I had with her.

Not long after that I got a phone call from her to tell me that she had given Neville's coin collection to Jamie, Alan's son. I had kept the coins for nineteen years and carried on collecting them. After Neville was killed, Mother kept all his stuff so that Alan could have first choice when he returned from Tangiers. So the coins came to me as a reject from Alan anyway. What an evil cow! I was livid. I eventually split the coins up into what I considered to be mine and took the remainder up to her and told her she could shove the box sideways up where the sun don't shine. That was the last time I ever spoke to her. I took the remaining coins to the charity shop as I wanted nothing more to do with them. It became apparent to me that my mother would sit and soak up every episode of Coronation Street on the TV and knew everything

182

each character was up to, but she hadn't the slightest clue nor interest in what was going on within her own family.

My sister Carolyn asked me to give her and her children a lift up to my mother's one Sunday months later. I knew that she and my other sister, Christine, went regularly for Sunday lunch. My mother was mortally embarrassed when she looked out of the door and saw me. "You can have some lunch," she said. I told her that I would rather go to the pub and eat my lunch with people I like. That was the last time I saw her. Now she is in a care home with Alzheimer's and doesn't recognise anyone. I haven't seen her for 20 years and have no intentions of seeing her nor going to her funeral. She ran out on me back in 1979, has never been there for me, so let the old bitch rot!

Aunty Dorothy, her sister, keeps telling me, "She's still your mother," and it means not one jot to me. As far as I am concerned, she has always been a nonentity in my life. I am not sad nor bitter about it, it's a fact!

It soon became apparent what stress I had been under all these years. I remember when I started getting stomach ulcers shortly after Father walked out and they got worse after Neville was killed. I got piles and would joke that the only thing I inherited from my father was his piles. After therapy I now realise that I didn't inherit them, they are a direct result of the poor eating habits and lack of self-esteem brought on by inconsiderate parents. All five of us were just a by-product of their love making, that was apparent. I have the discharge letter from hospital when I was five, and it reads:

Sedgefield General Hospital. 29th November 1960.

Dear Doctor Beveridge,

This little boy has been discharged. He was fully investigated and in spite of our fears I am very pleased to say

183

that all he was suffering from was probably iron deficiency, anaemia, probably due to malnutrition. He was seen by the Paediatrician, Dr Welsh from West Hartlepool, and he agreed with me that it was a Henach's purpura, as we had already talked about previously, but nevertheless we had to exclude leukaemia and this has been done satisfactorily. He was kept in much longer because he picked up a lot of infection on the ward.

I got that letter from my doctor a few months ago and stood and cried when I read it. It's one thing to suspect that you were neglected but it's another thing to have it confirmed in writing.

I am not blaming my parents for events that have happened, I am blaming them for their total lack of interest in our wellbeing throughout our lives. I have scraped the surface of who they are and where they have come from but I am not about to make excuses for them and the way they were brought up. I do however have extremely strong views about how children are raised, hopefully with love and consideration and guidance, not left like wild beings as we were. But this has had its advantages too.

What therapy did for me was to look objectively at my life and start joining up the pieces to make a big picture and what made me what I am today. I have depth and integrity and I am proud that I have. I have had the balls to look back at my life and make sense of it. Some people go through the whole of their lives afraid to look or don't have to look. It came as quite a shock to me that the suicidal feelings I was having, were that I would rather have died than look at the cause. And none of it was my fault. It is a normal human reaction to turn things in on yourself and blame yourself. It's not normal to start doubting your family. You are taught all your life to love and respect your parents.

Going back to the start of this book and my total disrespect for my parents, I will let you decide if they deserve it.

To summarise, I had run away from the break-up of our family and the death of Neville for so long that it was nigh on impossible to look back at it. It took great courage and strength of character to overcome it, and going back to Neville's death, your body takes over and protects you from such massive trauma. Look at getting Father out of my head in therapy. Locked in so tight that I didn't even realise it was there.

Parents

They fuck you up your mam and dad
They may not mean to but they do
They fill you with the faults they had
and some extra just for you
But they were fucked up in their turn
By fools in old style hats and coats
Who half the time were soppy stern
And half at one another's throats
Man hands on misery to man
It deepens like a coastal shelf
Get out as early as you can,
And don't have any kids yourself.

Philip Larkin. April 1971

And the last word on the matter, Therapy, for me, gave me a new way to think about things, a way to grasp what had happened and a way to cope with the truth.

I am mostly glad that I did it, but with a few reservations. Once you pop you can't stop. I analyse everything now and can see things that a lot of other people can't. It's almost as if I now have access to parts of my brain that I never previously had.

And the biggest negative is best described as an emotional ladder. Every stress you have to endure in life, death, divorce, loss etc, pushes you up a rung (or two) on the emotional ladder. The more you have endured, the higher up you are. I joke that I am teetering on the top! So people who have had very few stress levels in their lives become tedious, they put so much emphasis onto the tiniest of mishaps and are very difficult for me to relate to. They irritate me to death. When I say that I don't do petty in any way, shape or form, I mean these people. You're upset that you broke a nail,

GET A LIFE!!

The emotional ladder allows you to empathise with the people on the lower rungs but your real sympathy goes to anyone on the rungs above. People who have had bigger trauma than yourself.!

These days I can't watch TV if there is any interaction between a father and son. It breaks my heart. Goodnight Mister Tom is a prime example. Overall, my father was a shadow in the background figure who beat us up at mother's bidding, when he came in from work, for misdemeanours earlier in the day. I never saw any show of affection from him and I am sure that in his tiny mind he thought that any show of affection would make me queer, when in fact the opposite is the truth. I must stress at this point that the facts in this book and the events are as 'I' encountered them. My brother and sisters will have seen it and experienced it in their own way. My parents are totally responsible for not providing the emotional support that I needed. I blame their misjudgement for me not being able to have a loving committed relationship. I was happy to have affairs with foreigners as that wasn't the real life. Madge and Roy provided the roof over our heads and the basics but child rearing should have love and support and nurturing. Instead we got any self-esteem knocked out of us with the belt, slipper, poker, riding crop.

Remember at the beginning of this book I was going to call it 'A Journey in the Dark', well, the dark became the light after Therapy and I can look forward to a bright and happy future with no demons on my shoulders weighing me down. I can still get extremely upset if I allow myself to dwell on the past or if I speak about it but I am happy in the knowledge that it is all behind me.

A point to note is that during therapy I never discussed anything with anyone but phoned Madge to find out how long I had been in hospital when I was 5. Her usual response of, "Oh, I don't know," was followed with, "You should have a wife to discuss these things with." What a cow!

Chapter 14

Post-Therapy

The first thing I realised after therapy was that I had absolutely no respect for my parents. Having been brought up to love and respect your parents. How could I when the biggest grief I have endured throughout my life was completely due to the tiny minds and totally self-centred attitudes of both my parents. Aunty Dorothy used to say, when I was slagging my mother off, "Well, she is still your mother." MOTHERS in my mind, nurtured and encouraged their offspring, pointed them in the right direction and wanted only the very best for their children. Not Madge, she was ME, ME, ME all the way, she came first, second and last in everything. My sisters were nurtured by Madge, but as this ridiculous British system of separating the girls from the boys dictated, Madge had no idea how to deal with boys, even though she had two brothers. So poor Aunty Dorothy took a lot of convincing that Madge may hold the title of being mother but she certainly never displayed any of the qualities.

A very interesting fact that reared up years later was that Granny Jopling was exactly the same as Madge, self-centred, and nowadays Carolyn my sister has been displaying the same characteristics. Let's take Granny first. Uncle Alan being the youngest of the Jopling's was last to leave home, but at 18 years of age he went into the Army and got posted to Malta. He sent his money home regularly for Etty to bank for him. Imagine his surprise when he got back and there was no money left. She had treated herself to meals out, gone to the Cinema and shopping in Stockton. So Madge only looks like Aunty Margaret but was really her mother through and through. Carolyn on the other hand helped herself to £68,000 from Ken Smith's bank account whilst he lay dying in hospital. She got his credit card and bank book on 1st July 2009 when he was admitted to hospital and she went every day for forty days and drew out £300 using his credit card and by the time he died in October the same year, four months later, she had written two cheques out for £25,000, and she still maintains it was a gift. Ken's will clearly states that he left all his money to Madge. What callous selfish cows! (All three of them.)

Therapy didn't stop just because I didn't go to the sessions anymore. My head and intellect kept me analysing for around six years afterwards. These days I don't have anything to do with my siblings and I haven't spoken to Madge since the "Neville's coins" incident years ago. Whilst it is liberating not to be tied down with family and all the commitments that go along with having one, I realise that whilst travelling abroad I had unconsciously been seeking out "A NEW FAMILY". The Munoz family in Spain, The Sgouros family in Crete. The farm has always been my second family and these days they are my first. Mother Wilkinson (Doreen) was a wonderful mother who always put her family and their interests first. She provided for them wholeheartedly. I am proud to say that she took me in and treated me like one of her own, she was a

189

wonderful woman, and remained so right up to her death in 2011.

During my time abroad I would talk about the farm as my home. The shame of what my parents had done was still bottled in so tight that if was far preferable to talk about the farm as home. I still to this day go up and help out whenever I can. It was at the 21st birthday party of Robbie, Keith's youngest son, that I realised what thoroughly nice people they all were, and reflected later on how things could have panned out so much better for me if I had stayed on the farm and not run away abroad.

Aunty Dorothy told me recently that She and Madge were "not wanted" when Etty married her second husband. They got palmed off on aunts and uncles and eventually went into the Wrens. When they came home, they went to Aunty Margaret's. So when Madge married Ken Smith and went to live with him, it was "normal" for her to abandon the rest of us, because her mother had done that to her.

I wrote more poetry during the six years that I was doing therapy, some good, some bad and some indifferent. A good friend of mine suggested that I was purging myself from the shite I had carried around for years. HOW TRUE!

The World Today

There's a world beyond your garden gate, way down beyond your street,

Don't live your life as others do, afraid themselves they'll meet.

Get out and go and meet yourself in the world beyond the sea,

Push out your chest and say to all, "There's nothing wrong with me!"

It's easy to be lethargic and live as others do,

Difficult to confront yourself and see who's really you.

The realms beyond the grey North Sea teach better understanding,

Allowing their folks to be open minds, not twisted, under-handing.

Family life is to be revered, friendships cherished till they're strong,

Give your hearts to all who come, till they have done you wrong,

Animals have their rights too, they are here for a reason,

Cruelty to them in any form is nothing short of treason.

There's beauty in this isle of ours, green as it may be,

There's radiance in the hearts of those who have seen beyond the sea,

You've got to go and look yourself, just to appreciate what I mean,

So don't stay narrow minded and don't offer advice until you've been!

The Life of an Aged Holiday Rep

I used to live a great life, living wild and free,

Roaming all around the world and never knowing who's me,

I had a marvellous lifestyle with friends from near and far,

There's not a soul on this here earth could live life on a par,

The wisdom that it taught me, the lessons that I learned,

A hedonistic lifestyle never should be spurned,

I still have most of the friends I made along the way,

I only wish we could be as close to this very day,

Life goes off at tangents, folk wander here and there,

It's forward all the way with never a backward stare,

I've met myself and pondered deep on what made me this way,

A coward I am for not looking before to be sorted before today,

I had a very rough passage when I was 23,

Family problems in too short a time, but none the fault of me,

The leaving of my father on Christmas Eve did hurt,

He wanted to spend his Christmas with his latest bit of skirt,

His eldest daughter idolised him so two suicide attempts ensued,

Our life over as a family, resentment now accrued,

My youngest brother Neville, was 21 in March,

No card or word from Father; his severance was starch,

On 29th of September, he met his untimely end,

At 21, a very young age and killed by his best school friend,

I had to identify him, no father to do the task,

The horror still passes through me, you'll never know, don't ask.

In the midst of all these troubles, I had my first gay affair,

A handsome solicitor from Newcastle, he really made me stare,

I always thought I was the only one with the affliction of fancying men,

I only wish my knowledge now had helped me way back then,

Gay affairs in this isle of ours are done and over quickly,

I only wish my new affair hadn't ended whilst I was sickly,

His remorse for his boyfriend before me, made him suicidal,

Another weight to drag me down, attached to me like a bridle,

I lost the plot, I couldn't go on, the pressure exploding my head,

What had I done to deserve this crap, I was really better off dead,

I stood on the 11th storey balcony, my head was split in two,

The devil and the deep blue sea were fighting out what I should do,

If I had never made that phone call, the police would never have arrived,

Now here 25 years on, I am glad that I survived.

Chapter 15

Spiritual Healing

Closure on Neville's death came about in a very peculiar and unexpected way. I was at home in Cleasby when I suddenly, from nowhere, decided that I needed to go to the Spiritual Church. I have never been religious and have never really felt the need to go to church. However, I had this overwhelming need to go to the Spiritual Church. I told a friend Barbara, my dentist's mother, and she agreed to come with me. She had been before. We went to the one in Darlington, one Saturday evening. I had made my mind up that I was going with a completely open mind. Imagine my horror when the first Medium up on the stage said, "I have a song going through my head: You are the first, my last, my everything, by Barry White, can anyone take it?" I sat there stunned, it was Neville's favourite song, he used to play it nonstop. I knew because I shared a bedroom with him. I wasn't convinced that she wanted to talk to me so I kept quiet. She chatted on around the room to people and I was beginning to get the feel of what was expected when she pointed directly at me and said, "YOU! I have a James coming through." I nearly died of shock and started crying immediately. He was James Neville but we always called him Neville. She then waffled on about he liked a pint of lager with his mates and proceeded to name them one by one, John, Des etc. How the hell was she doing this? Especially, coming out with the name Des. The closing sentence was, "He is fine, he is with his grandmothers now and they are taking good care of him!" That's all I needed, just that sentence, but Christ it was spooky. I did go a couple more times but nothing could come close to that first night.

Even after therapy, you still continue to analyse things and it's an amazing tool and comes up with some eureka moments.

When I got Murphy the horse in 2006 and kept him at a farm in the next village. Wendy the farmer's wife asked if I would like to ride out with her one day. I got Murphy saddled up and ready to go and it wasn't until I was actually up on his back, waiting for Wendy, that I realised, what's the rush? I had to be on his back before Wendy. That was tantamount! It was the abandonment thing again. If she had been mounted first and ridden off leaving me behind, I couldn't bear it. So once you have gained the power you can put it to rights. I don't allow myself to be so upset now and can manage the feelings.

My strong beliefs about child rearing, even though I have never had any myself, have been strengthened by my past and also a great belief that children are mini adults and should be treated as such. They need two parents as role models but from two years old, when they naturally start being independent, they should be guided into self-discovery projects to bring out their natural talents. Unlike us, we were just abandoned and as long as we were out of the house, out of Madge's way, that suited her fine.

I am going to stick my neck out here and be brave and quote one of my findings. They are MY findings and if you don't believe in them, then I challenge you to challenge your beliefs. Whilst travelling abroad in the Med, where family life is the absolute essence of life, and two or sometimes three generations live within the same house. Everyone within that house knows who they are and what their role is in life. The whole family look after the children and they in turn grow up to be well rounded, balanced human beings. You don't get nearly as many screwballs as you do in this country. For example, I know of a mother who would rather have a spray tan and false eyelashes than feed her three-year-old daughter. She reads Hello magazine and truly believes that she lives that lifestyle. I call her Fuckwit but she was abandoned by her mother, brought up by her grandparents and is totally narcissistic.

Taking this one step further, to rile you up even more. The English way of sending kids to boarding school at age 8 is absolutely heartless and shameful. Pushing your kids away, before they are fully developed. I have a lot of ex public school friends and the reason we get on so well, and what we all have in common is that we were abandoned as children. My mate Harry went to Fetty's in Edinburgh and has told me that his dad used to meet him from the train when he was eight years old and shake his hand. He'd been at school for months, he needed a hug! I must admit that after working in the Med for eleven years and coming back to Britain, I do find the English cold and heartless. EG just like my parents!

Closure from Kevin

Here I am sitting in 2012 writing this book and it was only last week that whilst driving through Wensleydale, coming down a steep bank and stopping at a T junction, that out of nowhere the thought jumped into my head, "I forgive you Kevin." Now where did that come from? It was a beautiful day, I was admiring the scenery coming up to Redmire and like a bolt out of the blue, BANG! It came into my head. I think it is a brilliant example of how your conscious mind and sub conscious mind are connected. I have used the technique for years that if something is troubling me and I can't work it out, I walk away from it. Bin it! The solution ALWAYS appears in your head without any effort from yourself. And like this example, there was no semblance of Kevin to bring it to mind.

I had spent years believing that Kevin would come back. How could such an idyllic summer together come to an abrupt stop? He would surely realise eventually and come back to me. How wrong I was and how downright stupid I had been to believe it. Kevin was a user through and through. He had used Jimmy his ex to get ahead in the housing market and then dumped him and run in the most cowardly fashion. I was a willing accomplice in the matter too I am ashamed to say. He then used me to keep out of the situation by staying with me for 8 months of the summer and all the while stealing from me. He was stealing my cigarettes, petty I know but I ignored it. He was mortified when I asked him to claim some rent off his company to help me pay the flat in Soufouli Street. And then BINGO I hit on the reason he could never come back. Two cheques had been stolen from my briefcase in Gibraltar and I blamed everyone possible but not Kevin. It had to be him, he was the only one with access to it when it was in the apartment in Gibraltar Beach.

Imagine the catastrophe if I had complied and bought property with him. My inner voice had told me to beware and I am so pleased to this day that I never went along with him. I have tried on many occasions to contact Kevin, even been to Ellesmere Port looking for him but my feelings today are that I hope he gets everything he deserves in this life.

Chapter 16

Present Day

These days I don't suffer fools gladly, I don't do petty in any way shape or form. Reality is what counts in this life, as far as I am concerned. I am me, a whole person, not a part of my job nor car. I remember when I first got back from London in 1994 and I was in a bar in town. I was asked what sort of car I drive, I replied, "One that is paid for, why?" I really cannot see what relevance a type of car has on my credibility as a person. I drive what suits me! It may not suit everyone else but who cares. If you want to drive a BMW or Mercedes that sits on the drive for weeks in icy weather, that's up to you. My car is cost effective, practical and does me for all my needs.

Before I went abroad, I had a very privileged social circle. My friends were all farmers' sons and daughters, or business owner's offspring. I was lucky to have them and had a brilliant social life. Here I am thirty years on and I haven't got time for most of them. Trust fund kids! Everything handed to them on a plate. No depth and no character. Pointless lives. A lot of them have wasted their lives waiting for their inheritance, some crippled by ageing parents who dictate that no partner is good enough for them, so I have a lot of single friends. They really aren't worth bothering with. Let them stew in their tiny lives, embittered with their inability to have a relationship or a real life. Some are gay and married, living the life that is expected of them rather than be true to themselves, living the lie. Poor sad lot!

I went to a joint sixtieth birthday and new house warming party a few years ago. It was a scorching hot day so I rolled up in my stylish cotton shorts, a smart cotton shirt, open collared, and sandals. Only to get there and find the fuddy-duddy brigade were out in force. Middle class fuckwits, in long sleeved shirts done up to the collar and with a tie on, long trousers, shoes and socks. Jokingly I asked the hosts if they would like me to go home and change. No, they said, so and so is coming in his shorts. Yes, there was another man turned up in a pair of khaki shorts down to his knees, I am sure they were ex-army or Boy Scouts. By far the best part was when I went over to speak to two old hunting pals, Jane and Beverley. Jane was dressed as if she had fallen into the laundry basket at a charity shop and come out wearing whatever stuck, whether it fit or not. The sun hat was 1930s and washed out. The dress must have been at least six times too big for her and again pre-war and washed out. Jane proceeded to publicly humiliate me about being overweight. Don't these people ever look at themselves I thought. I got away from them and thought not my scene anymore. It was twice the insult as it was just a couple of weeks beforehand when I had alerted Jane to a hole in her fence where a car had gone through and I knew there were three horses in the field. I certainly won't be doing any favours for that bitch again.

I have evolved in my lifetime. Not stagnated like a lot of English. I am still crippled by the past and struggle to justify some issues, but I have the rest of my life to muse over them. This book has been a godsend to purge my system. It's like putting the lid on the past. I do, however, get mortified by people's stupidity.

I recently went to a wedding in a church up near Durham. Ralph from the farm came up to me in the church, after the service, and started to ridicule me publicly about being fat. I stood there and said nothing. People who I had been talking to were walking away with embarrassment. Even Ralph's wife looked mortified. All I could think about was, I am just fat, I can do something about that, you! will be an arsehole all your life! I personally would be mortified to knowingly hurt somebody's feelings. I have learned enough in life to realise that there could be an underlying reason why someone is fat, be it emotional, mental, whatever. Remember Ralph is only six months older than me. What a spineless weak man he has turned out to be!

Having lived abroad for so long, I can't think like these people, I can't be superficial and narrow minded. I often say to friends "You are being very English" when they are struggling to come to terms with something I have said, or done. What gets me really wound up is the ones who know the least, they are the ones who fight their corner the hardest. As I have said before in this book, I am not out to change anyone, I only fight my corner when challenged.

Still Living It Large

I am still a bit wild and thrive on new experiences. I went down to Leicestershire to drive fast cars a few years ago. I drove a Lamborghini at 130 MPH, a Ferrari at 130 MPH but then the instructor took me round the same track at 150 MPH, now that was a white-knuckle ride. I took a Lotus Caterham round at 110 MPH and the instructor had told me it would do 130 MPH, so when I questioned it and got told it was because of my extra weight, I could have spit! I realised at the time that I was only driving the Lambo to spite my father. He would have been in cloud nine if he had ever got the chance to drive one. I even pointed my middle finger up to heaven and said "Fuck you Roy", I realise that he probably isn't in heaven anyway if you want to believe that bolony.

Revelations

I have had many revelations about things from the past and how they have affected me in later life. I think that everyone should think about their actions and how it affects others. I for one have a mortal fear of being left behind due to the abandonment. I remember vividly getting off the ferry from Rhodes to Turkey, in Marmaris, and struggling with my luggage, Kevin was walking ahead of me and the panic going through me was horrendous. I can control it now to a certain extent but it does pop up now and again. I get frustrated with people, especially women, who put themselves before their children, resulting in the child suffering (like I did). A friend of mine's wife is so lazy and stupid that her son, now 21, has the most diverse eating habits. When he was young and she put something out for him to eat that he didn't like, instead of finding things that he did like, she insisted that he ate what he didn't like. Resulting in a young man with severe eating disorders and worse still, she takes NO responsibility for it.

My time spent abroad taught me that families are the basis of any social group and for example in Greece where there are three generations living in the same house, everyone knows their role and contributes to the smooth running of the family and a stronger bond between extended family members. I am a firm believer that children are mini adults and should be treated like persons rather than be beaten into submission like we were. Children who are brought up to be responsible, grow up to be responsible adults. I cannot stress how irritated I get when speaking to senior citizens here in the UK and they are twittering on like everything is everybody else's fault. They aren't responsible for anything. Worse still is listening to Politicians, what mind bendingly tedious individuals they are. Never meet a question head on. Ducking and diving with their answers. They must have spaghetti for brains.

One thing that therapy has left me with is an utter intolerance of petty! Old people who never take responsibility for their actions boil my piddle. Twining on about something and blaming others. I tell them straight.

I meet every problem with the same opinion, it's never insurmountable. It may take some thinking about to solve, but I am not going to lose sleep to get past it. Gone are the days when I was a teenager going to a horse show and couldn't sleep for all the things that could go wrong going full gallop around my brain. "Se la vie" and "Que Sara"!

Another story has just sprung to mind about when I was a teenager. Late teens, I think. I had been show jumping up at Stannington in Northumberland and had won two rosettes and was feeling well pleased with myself, BUT on reaching home with the rosettes in my pocket, I never even told Madge or Roy, they wouldn't have cared less. Now isn't that sad?

Chapter 17

The Last Chapter

So, all of my life experiences have affected me in one way or another. I still suffer from abandonment to the extreme where I can't (won't) have a close relationship for fear of the hurt that it entails. I could never entrust my feelings to anyone. I am very sad that I was denied the right to a relationship due to circumstances. Wanda and Manolis were the nearest I got to a lasting relationship but due to it being pre therapy, it was never going to happen. I thought Kevin was the one I wanted to spend the rest of my life with but after the long arduous task of getting him straight in my head I decided that he would never have made the grade. Had my parents not been so stupid, heartless and self-centred and had taken the task of having children on in a mature and responsible manner, then things would have turned out quite different and I would not be writing this book. Have I been over sensitive, am I over sensitive? I will let you decide

My parents were brought up in the age where boys and girls were kept separate (as it was in my junior school). So in our household my mother was always there for the girls but didn't know how to deal with the boys, so we were left to our own devices. Father being out at work all the time. I give him that, he was a good provider. Mind you he could have worked a bit less if Fat Madge hadn't stuffed her fat gob so much. The fact that he ran away when I was five and in hospital, leaving a wife and five kids to fend for themselves, makes him lacking in something but I am not quite sure what. He had been the apple of his mother's eye, as the youngest of the family and she had spoilt him. BUT he had deserted them and never went back for years, so that is why we never met them until I was about ten years old. And then he went again when I was 23, he wanted to spend Christmas with his new girlfriend, can you believe the arrogance of the man? Christmas Eve, what a time to run out on your family, but then have the arrogance, to expect them to keep in touch afterwards.

I have suffered every stress related disease as a result of the careless actions of my parents. I started wetting the bed again after leaving hospital at 5 and did so until I was around 10 years old. I had stomach ulcers for years after Father ran off and Neville was killed. I got Bell's Palsy, and still have it, after doing therapy. And now at 57 years old I have developed Shingles.

I hate injustice, people suffering for something that is due to someone else's lack of foresight, stupidity or lack of care. I personally cannot abide to be accused of something I am not to blame for. I now know that it is because I carried the guilt of my brother's death around for 27 years, not knowing how to deal with it. I react very strongly if I get accused of something that isn't my fault and react extremely violently towards the perpetrators. I still feel other people's pain and tend to put others before myself, although this is getting addressed as I write this book. I am first now, everyone else comes afterwards.

As young as five years old, I worked hard at keeping everyone happy, being subservient, making things RIGHT! Just so that I wouldn't be abandoned again!

These days I go out of my way to help friends. The time, money and emotional strain I invest in people NEVER gets paid back. ALL due to being abandoned!

A friend said recently, "Would anyone think any the less of you if you didn't do it?"

That became another Eureka moment! The penny dropped! I don't need to buy something for a friend, then deliver it, and usually chase the money for payment.

That's just me, keeping relations sweet with my friends so that they won't let me down. I have been so busy all of my life, or at least since age five, doing just that. To the detriment of ME, when all the while, all I wanted, and still want, is someone to call mine!

I really cannot abide human stupidity and you only have to analyse the news on TV to see what absolute dickheads are running the country, large businesses etc. I thank the lord that I can see things as a whole and see what the consequences are for whatever actions.

A friend has just asked me why calves are kept apart from their mothers on farms. Well, if humans need the milk, who has to dip out??? The calves! It's not rocket science. Whilst I am on the subject, what kind of stupidity puts rules into action that condemns the life of bull calves on dairy farms. They are shot at birth because they don't produce the best quality meat that meets the human guidelines. It's intolerable. All animals have a right to life, be it for human consumption or otherwise.

Here's a theory for you to think about. Children in the UK are brought up to believe in Fairies and Father Christmas etc.

How about teaching them the realities of life right from the beginning, so that they can grow into well rounded adults with responsibility and integrity. Their mothers and fathers, hopefully with responsible attitudes and acting as role models, should be encouraged to bring up their own children, without greed and selfishness taking over. I am reliably informed and wholeheartedly agree that children's personalities are fully developed by the time they are two years old. I was brought up when children were to be seen but not heard. My parents in their own stupidity knocked any semblance of self-respect and faith in ourselves out of us from a very young age. Balanced well-adjusted children who grow into well-adjusted adults are surely a better option. These days my best friends are ex public school so had been abandoned in school from the age of 8, we share the same "psyche" to a greater or lesser effect.

I can't abide trust fund kids who treat the world like it is their playground and everything should come to them as a right, without working for it. I am glad that I have led a real life and not one that has depended on the good fortunes of others. I have friends who are working off massive mortgages to allow the other siblings to enjoy a comfortable life, as their birthright. Get out and work for it, it's doubly rewarding if you have toiled to achieve it. Everything you get for free in this life is worthless. FACT!!

I am very unreligious. When the Mormons come to the door, I like to have a real play with them. I fail to understand how anyone could come round to the door and preach religion when they have never once been to the Holy Land and seen what religion does to people. My favourite line to them, that my lifestyle would certainly not be tolerated by your religion.

I worked in Israel three times and I was far from impressed by the injustices that I saw, and coupled with the wars and fighting due to religion going on around the world, it all needs re writing. Any religion that condemns other human beings and other religions should be phased out. Small mindedness, to the extremes.

I have strong feelings about death and can deal with it now. I must tell you about Ella's husband's death to give you a better understanding. The Irish believe that when you die you go to a better life. I arrived in the village where Ella lives just as the hearse was heading down the village after dropping off the coffin. I very nearly baulked and ran. Remember I have avoided funerals for years. I feel people's pain and was not looking forward to seeing Ella upset. So I bit the bullet and braved it. I arrived at the house and let myself in to find Ella sat in the dining room by the coffin, with several others, wringing her hands and crying. I walked in quietly and sat by her and held her hand. I didn't know what to say. Suddenly her husband's cat, Jasper, jumped onto the window sill where there was a candle burning and set fire to itself. Ella's exclamation of, "Fuck me, the cat is trying to cremate itself!" That was it, the bubble burst and we all laughed and had a good piss up and dance to send Michael on his way.

So death to me now is the reality that we can all look forward to, nothing we can do about it and when it comes, BANG! It don't matter an ounce how much money you have or how many possessions or how much power, it's not going anywhere with you. Worm food is all you are worth!

On the whole I am pleased that I did therapy and I feel empowered by the knowledge and insights it has given me. There have been times when I wished that I hadn't bothered and had remained ignorant to the realities. My therapist told me that I was brave for looking as most people rattle through life and never face their demons. My power these days is that I can help people with their anxieties if I choose to do so. I don't push that there is a need to but if you are distressed enough, I will help you. Such is my nature. The downside is that I am teetering on the top of the emotional ladder and it really is tedious having to deal with people who are further down the ladder and who put far too much emphasis and emotion onto pointless idiotic matters. I call these people crippled with a tiny mind. I recently had a woman run into the back of my car and all she could harp on about after it was, what would have happened if my two-year-old son had been in the car. I shut her up by telling her that I had run away abroad for eleven years because my brother had been killed in a car accident. What a happy world we would live in if people lived a real life and removed "what if" from their existence.

I am far more forthright with the truth now and I have no problem whatsoever in telling folk what I think. The best one yet is when I say to people giving their own small-minded advice, "But I don't want to be like you!"

Thoughts from Recently

I never stood a chance in life. Being abandoned at 5 years old made me work harder at relationships, to be accepted. No matter how you look at it, being abandoned was turned in on myself and fuelled the need to be accepted. I don't think I was ever loved by my parents. We children were just a by-product of our parents' love. Madge cooked and cleaned for us but never showed outwardly that she cared. Not the boys anyway.

I have an intellectual mind which needs stimulating and Madge was hardly the best candidate to do that. Her passive nature irritated me to extremes. If you asked her a question, you obviously needed an answer. "Oh, I don't know!" was her usual response. Couldn't be bothered, wasn't interested. Coronation Street was on the TV. That was far more important.

We got kicked and screamed at for the smallest of demeanours. I remember Aunty Margaret arrived at the house in Aycliffe shortly after we moved there. So I will have been about ten years old. I was sitting on the floor and farted. Madge kicked me so hard I felt like she had broken my leg.

Looking back with a logical sense, I realise that I wanted to be Jai in the Tarzan films, even at that young age, as I needed a man in my life. Some big strong arms to protect me. A father, a role model. Roy could never do that though. He was the macho type. Men cuddling sons makes them Gay! Well, in actual fact, it's the opposite that makes them gay. Children need the love and affection of BOTH Parents, two role models, to become a whole person themselves!

I have tried over and over to summarise this book but I have had to walk away from it, so many times. This morning, Sunday 25th March 2019, I am sat at my computer typing for the last time, looking across the village green in the spring sunshine. I have decided that this is the last on the matter. I started crying before I started to type. Before I even engaged my mind! This book has been a godsend at bringing closure. I have to move on now. I really hope that you will forgive me for the waffle, in the last two chapters, that doesn't really conclude. I have done my absolute best so you shouldn't expect any more.

To all the People who Shine...

The people who shine and seem very bright,
with smiles on their faces and feet that are light,
are not always those who have walked in the sun,
but those who faced darkness fought it and won.

Aunty Dorothy died in 2013. I was due to go and decorate her bungalow and she rang and cancelled me because she wasn't feeling too well, but couldn't put a name to how she felt. The next thing she was taken into hospital. The following Sunday I was travelling up the A19 on my way back from work and the thought hit me, I have to go and see her. So I rerouted and headed for the Hospital. She was sitting up and chatting with Aunty Audrey and Uncle Ray. She was pleased that I had come. She died peacefully in her sleep that night. I wrote a poem for her which they read out at her funeral.

Aunty Dorothy

Died Monday 29th April, aged 85.
You have to have a legend in your life,
Someone, who is always there.
An angel in human form,
Now that is only fair.

Dorothy was always in my life,
Right from the very start.
Always there for me through thick and thin,
And I loved her right from the heart.

Her humour was akin to mine,
Bawdy and really quite shocking,
We used to laugh loud and long,
But never at anything mocking.

It saddens me to think she's gone,
To the great house up in the sky.
But Sunday night in the hospital,
I am glad I went to say bye-bye.

Aunty Dorothy, remembered with great pride at having
known you. x

A year later, I had a spooky experience. I was driving to work past Teesside Airport at 4am. It was dark but starting to be light, foggy patches and damp. All of a sudden, I saw a murky figure walk across the road and disappear. As it is a country road and no houses for miles, I was mystified. Only when regaling the story to Aunty Audrey did she highlight that it was the anniversary of Dorothy's death. 29th April!

Madge is in a nursing home and has been for the past 7 years. I have never seen her for years, certainly since well before I started writing this book, and I have no great need to go and see her. She has Dementia and doesn't know who anyone is. The woman who put a great big NOTHING into my wellbeing, future and career. Yes, she gave birth to me! After therapy I realised that in her little mind, my father only left her, not us. When Neville was killed, it only affected her, not us. So self-obsessed!

I went through a long time of hating her when I finished therapy and I think that is apparent at the start of this book. The book that jumped out of my head after therapy because it had festered there for far too long. Nowadays I feel nothing for her, she is a stranger that once I knew, but I am still very aware that I was abandoned at 5, missed the opportunity to go to Grammar School when I didn't take my 11 Plus exam. And just as I was starting my career, Father ran off. What a pair of losers. I can only thank them for the lack of self-worth, the persecution complex, and the fact that I could never have a relationship. Believe me when I tell you that all I ever craved in life was someone who could be mine!

I think the following paragraph sums her up nicely.

Beware of tiny minds, who live in gated communities and think their world is the only world. For they will band together like their forefathers and jump in their droves into the sea. Never having dipped their toes in the real world. And woe betide those who go through their gate.

HRP. January 2019.

Shirley Smith still remains my Top Girl. Even though she has been married twice, had two daughters, and now has five grandchildren. We still cause ructions where ever we go. We are on each other's wavelength. We recently watched an old 1940s' film at her house with the sound turned down. Shirley and I provided the dialogue. We cried with laughter. What a great game. I am sure that Ralph, her husband, thought we were completely bonkers.

Lastly, I remain single, it has been 30 years now. Living in Beautiful North Yorkshire and working flat out. I do a bit of support acting for a couple of agencies and love every minute of it. The best being my part in Victoria, I played a 1940s' sailor. I had the time of my life. What a brilliant experience!

This Quote Sums up Me in My Present Situation

"I am currently unsupervised, I know, it freaks me out too, but the possibilities are endless."

As I am no longer impressed with wealth and status, this quote is just how I view people these days.

The only sizes I'm interested in are the size of your heart, the width of your emotions, and the breadth of your intellect.

I would like to mention a great friend Julia Ellwood. I have known her since she was 8 years old. She is the one who fainted off her pony when I had the accident on Castle Hill and split my stomach open. We had some great times together with horses, on the beaches in Crete, at Hunt Balls. She was a man's woman, great fun and a great character. She could party like no one I have ever met before or since.

We were in Crete in about 1986, she was with a few of her friends in an apartment. I was living there, and some Dutch and Geordie friends of mine were there at the same time. We all met in a Taverna in Citro Platea and had a great long table of about 12 of us. Julia and Ginny were sitting opposite me at the table, when I mentioned that she had a very long face, and asked, "What's up?" She replied nothing but asked me to tweak her nipple. I reached over the table to do so but she whipped her top up to reveal a bare breast with a face drawn on it. The nipple was the nose, big eyes and smiley mouth. So funny! We called it Smiley and he had a good airing that night all over town.

Years after that Julia and I went to Crete on holiday, sometime in the 1990s, and we had Maz from Rhodes with us. The first night, we just went mad and had a brilliant night out, so the monster hangovers were in full swing the next day on Amiros Beach. We were all getting caught up on sleep whilst sunbathing and I woke up first. I got a bit bored, being the only one awake. Maz was laid on her front, topless, and being a dancer and choreographer, she had the perfect 5-foot 6-inch body, and very fit. She was wearing a G string. So I went into a dark-haired friend's handbag and pulled out her hairbrush, and teased out all the black hairs from it. I then inserted the hair ball into the crack of Maz' backside. And there it remained for over an hour. Gently swaying in the breeze. Lots of people were passing where we were laid en route to the Beach Bar, showers, toilets etc. I made a point of beckoning their gaze to Maz' arse. Most of them had a good laugh.

Julia died suddenly in 2017 of an asthma attack and heart attack, aged 57. I cried for a week and I am on the verge again writing this. She had two beautiful children by then George and Natalie. I wrote the following poem for her and Chris, her partner, read it out at her funeral.

Julia Margaret Ellwood

I owe it to Julia to write this poem,
A greater friend I have never known,
I have known her since she was nine or ten,
A brilliant character even then,
She told us how monkey's mate,
She saw it on TV when she stayed up late.

The adventures we had in our horsey days,
Make me laugh and cry in so many ways.
She rode a horse, same as she rode through life,
Total abandon, no stress, or strife.
Life was but a game to play,
A laugh, a journey, no time to pray.

In Crete we caused havoc wherever we went,
Partying and drinking but always a laugh,
No trouble, no ructions, just clean honest fun,
A laugh a minute until we were all done.
The Greeks they loved Julia wherever she'd be,
Kindred spirits, best buddies, beside the sea.

It saddens me now that she has gone,
A truly great friend that was second to none,
Fond memories will stay with me for the rest of my life,
May she continue to party in the afterlife.
Julia was an angel, with a heart to match,
A lifelong friend I was honoured to catch.

Howard R Potts. 30th July 2017.